TWO MIRACLES

*

La Nonne qui laissa son abbaie

Saint Valentin

TWO MIRACLES

*

La Nonne qui laissa son abbaie

Saint Valentin

*

edited from the manuscript
Paris, B.N., f.fr. 819–820

by

NIGEL WILKINS

Lecturer in French,
University of St. Andrews

Published in the U.S.A. 1973 by:
HARPER & ROW PUBLISHERS INC.
BARNES & NOBLE IMPORT DIVISION

ISBN 06-497678-5

Printed in Great Britain by R. & R. Clark Ltd, Edinburgh

CONTENTS

PLATES

INTRODUCTION

1. THE MIRACLES DE NOTRE DAME

If it were not for the forty Miracles of Our Lady, we would know very little about the development of drama in fourteenth-century France. Between the fairly substantial repertory of liturgical and bourgeois plays of the thirteenth century[1] and the great flowering of Passion plays,[2] Sotties and Farces[3] in the fifteenth century, little remains to show us what was happening on the French stage in the intervening years, even though many external references make it clear that the fourteenth century, despite the trouble and turmoil of the Hundred Years War, was a period of exciting development and vigorous activity in the dramatic art, particularly in and around Paris.

The Miracle plays thus form a collection of particular significance especially when we find that their composition was not restricted to a single moment in time, but spans the years from 1339 to 1382. They were, in fact, composed for annual presentation by the Guild of the Goldsmiths of Paris and members of the Guild probably put them on as part of the festivities connected with the election of officers, which usually took place in December, There was a poetry competition too, and the winning pieces at this *puy* or gathering, in the form of *serventois* in honour of the Virgin, were often included in the manuscript collection together with the play of the same year. The subject matter of these poems reflects the religious theme of the plays and this is further emphasized by the presence of short sermons, sometimes preceding, sometimes worked into the plays themselves.

By and large, though one cannot generalize, the Miracles tended to increase in length as the years passed, and to become more elaborate in their use of stage equipment, more demanding in scenic variation. Most of the plays show how the Virgin, in her infinite mercy, comes to save or intercede for a sinner who, in a moment of extreme distress, calls upon her grace. The greater the sinner, the more glorious his eventual redemption. However, despite their similarity of purpose and certain

[1] E.g. *Le Jeu d'Adam*; Jean Bodel's *Le Jeu de Saint Nicolas*; Rutebeuf's *Le Miracle de Theophile*; Adam de la Hale's *Le Jeu de Robin et de Marion*.

[2] E.g. those by Arnoul Greban and Jean Michel.

[3] E.g. *La Farce de Maistre Pathelin*.

stock procedures in style, the forty Miracle plays vary very considerably in atmosphere and accomplishment. The substance for the plots is drawn from a number of contrasting sources: traditional and legendary miracles said to have been performed by the Virgin (e.g. No. 7 *La Nonne qui laissa son abbaie*; No. 15 *L'enfant ressucité*); Saint's Lives (e.g. No. 25 *Saint Valentin*; No. 40 *Saint Alexis*); episodes from epic or romance (e.g. No. 31 *Berthe, femme du roi Pepin*; No. 33 *Robert le Diable*); versions of historical legends (e.g. No. 13 *L'empereur Julien et Libanius*; No. 39 *Le baptême de Clovis*). In some examples a particular tendency towards realism is evident; in others the religious theme is strongly marked. The two plays chosen for the present edition, *La Nonne qui laissa son abbaie* and *Saint Valentin*, show these features respectively, and display well the great versatility of the various anonymous authors, who manage brilliantly to ring the changes on their basic material: from mediaeval France to ancient Rome.

2. LA NONNE QUI LAISSA SON ABBAIE (1345)

A nun, pious but beautiful, is persistently courted by a knight. At length she succumbs, promises to elope from the abbey and to marry her wealthy and dashing suitor. For two nights, as she attempts to leave, the Virgin bars her way; the third night the nun makes no obeisance to the Virgin's statue and is free to go. Many years of happy marriage ensue and two sons are born. After thirty years, however, when the knight has returned from a ten-year absence fighting for his overlord, the Virgin delivers an ultimatum: the nun must repent her sin or face the fires of hell. She returns to the abbey to finish her days in penance and the knight, equally stricken with remorse, becomes a monk.

The nun's first reluctance and subsequent surrender as her woman's instincts get the better of her are skilfully handled, as are her terror and tortured conscience when the enormity of her sin comes home to her. The knight, too, undergoes some character development, from an impassioned and reckless youth to a mature and generous *seigneur* in his middle age. We must remember that to the characters in the play and to the mediaeval audience the nun's fall from grace and the risk she runs of facing eternal damnation are of serious consequence, and that there is real dramatic tension beneath the surface as the years pass by on stage, each one confirming the error of her ways. The final parting of the couple, we may imagine, is a moment of great pathos, but followed swiftly by the greater glory of sin redeemed and the triumphant procession singing the hymn, *Veni Creator Spiritus*.

Into the bare framework are woven a number of extra scenes not essential to the plot, but immeasurably enhancing with their realistic touches the verisimilitude of the action, not to mention the sheer entertainment: the detail of the nuns' meal in the refectory; the sermon and antiphonal reponses in the chapel; the journey to the greater castle and the dramatic arrival of the messenger; the minstrels' playing during the banquet; the celestial singing of the angels. Minor characters, too, assume rounded proportions and, with the possible exception of the maidservant, are well assimilated into the structure of the play: the gracious and forgiving abbess; the amicable prioress; the reliable and devoted squire, always ready to serve, to give sound advice and, in the end, to attend to the domestic detail of the two abandoned children; the two sons themselves, the first older and more responsible, the second young and panic-stricken at the loss of his parents, but soon pacified by the thought of an apple from his uncle!

3. SAINT VALENTIN (1367)

Cato, the wisest man in Rome, has a son who is afflicted by an unpleasant and seemingly incurable paralytic disease. On the advice of one of his students, Cato sends for Valentine, renowned for the miraculous cures he has performed in Nervie. Valentine comes, cures the son and converts the household to Christianity. Among Cato's students is the Emperor's son, and when this young man expounds his new-found Christian beliefs before his pagan father, there is a furious reaction. Three fellow students and Valentine himself are beheaded, but not before news comes that most of the population has been converted to christianity, as God had promised the saint. The Emperor dies in agony with a fish-bone stuck in his throat and is dragged to hell by devils, while angels bear the martyred Valentine to paradise.

The atmosphere here is very different from that of *La Nonne qui laissa son abbaie*. Apart from the change in setting, the religious element is clearly very much more strongly emphasized. The main criticism that might be levelled by a modern reader is that the preaching aspect is preponderant. But we must remember that the main purpose of the Miracle plays is religious and that the occasion on which they were performed by the Goldsmith's Guild was at least semi-religious, if not wholly religious. The erudite sermon which precedes *Saint Valentin* finds its echoes in the saint's own preaching to Cato and to the Emperor and in the exposition of the Emperor's son; much importance is attached here to underlining, even at the risk of excessive repetition, the essentials of the Christian faith: the virgin birth; the nature of the Trinity; the *credo*. We are in an age when the crusading spirit was not yet dead and there is true dramatic tension in the saint's efforts to convert the pagans: it is the battle of good versus evil or, in mediaeval eyes, of right versus wrong. Moreover, the author is careful to juxtapose the heavier preaching and debating scenes with scenes of colourful or violent action; Cato the scholar is not completely convinced by learned argument, but won over by the miracle of his son's restoration to health; the debate before the Emperor is immediately followed by the beheading of the three students and their salvation by Notre Dame and her angels; Valentine's final avowal of his faith in Christ is combined with his being flogged at the stake, beheaded and borne to Heaven, while devils seize the suffocated Emperor and the grisly jailer. It is evident from this that the presentation of the play should bring out contrasts between moments of solemn and dignified beauty and those which are fast-moving, brutal – or even sometimes humorous in a grim kind of way.

Entertainment and interest is further provided by the colourful characters of the pagan camp, directly opposed to the dignity and perfection of the Christians and scholars. In the Palace of Rome, oaths always invoke pagan gods: Mahomet, Appolin; gruesome brutality is the order of the day. The despotic and self-centred Emperor holds sway over his court: the supercilious Chevalier; the two officious sergeants falling over themselves to please and keen to amuse themselves in the torture chamber, while disclaiming responsibility for the prisoner; the twisted jailer, most colourful of all and reminiscent of Bodel's Durant, so proud of his technique in tying prisoners up, in torture and in execution.

The general structure of the play also lends cohesion and dramatic interest: God's reply to Valentine's initial prayer anticipates the final conversion of the people of Rome; Valentine's speech in Cato's house prepares the converts for the trials to come; there is balance in the way in which the fourth and fifth students go on the early mission to Valentine and are there to accompany him at the end, while the first, second and third students play a central part in their martyrdom; the appearances of Notre Dame and her angels, this time at God's direct command, are characteristically balanced early and late in the play; two devils oppose the two angels. The techniques of linking and suspense are managed well; the celestial music is heard by the unseeing Emperor as the beheading scenes and angelic procession are skilfully interlocked; there is suspense in the withholding of the Saint's name (until line 170): in the miraculous curing of Cato's son; in the Saint's martyrdom – and, indeed, in the whole underlying plot of whether or not the pagans will be won over. The final hymn, in triumph as always, marks the undoubted victory of the Christian faith.

4. VERSIFICATION AND THE RONDEAUX

The Miracles are written throughout in the conventional form of octosyllabic rhyming couplets. The last line of every speech, however, with very few exceptions, is half-length, four syllables only, and rhymes with the first line of the following speech. The reason for this is probably that the shorter line was a useful cue. easily recognizable by its changed rhythm, thereby warning the next speaker to follow on. This means that every speech has to have at least one whole line to precede the half-line; there are none shorter. Lines are very seldom split between characters (a rare example is *Saint Valentin*, l. 1), the mark of a rather inflexible technique, but are occasionally broken by some obvious action or change of position on the stage (e.g. *La Nonne . . .*, ll. 198, 593; *Saint Valentin*, ll. 1201, 1215). However, the lines have a natural and sometimes even colloquial flow which reassures us that we are in the hands of a master; enjambement is used, much more in *Saint Valentin* than in *La Nonne . . .* (e.g. *La Nonne . . .*, ll. 316–317, 573–574, 741–742; *Saint Valentin*, ll. 27–28, 58–59, 64–65 etc.).

A characteristic of all the Miracles is the introduction of *Rondeaux*, mostly sung by the two archangels Gabriel and Michiel as they escort the Virgin from and back to Heaven. This feature of the Miracles in particular was taken up and widely exploited in the fifteenth century in Passions and Farces. The text leaves no doubt that these *Rondeaux* are to be sung and[1] also seem to indicate that the setting is in two-part harmony. Sadly (and strangely) no musical notation is included in any fourteenth- or fifteenth-century dramatic source and so we have to conjecture what the setting could be. It seems most likely that these *Rondeaux*, all in praise of the Virgin, are *contrafacta* or new texts based on pre-existent secular poems, sung to pre-existent music copied on separate sheets, probably with the secular verses still attached. Musical settings of religious Rondeaux in the fourteenth century are extremely scarce: *En tes doulx flans plains de virginité*[2] is one of the few known examples. A Miracle *Rondeau* using a similar metrical scheme[3] could be

---

[1] E.g. *La Nonne . . .*, ll. 320–327, 418–425, 843–848, 876–882; *Saint Valentin*, ll. 321–329, 353–356, 1028–1030, 1039–1040, 1062–1063, 1069–1088.

[2] Ed. W. Apel, *French Secular Music of the fourteenth Century*, Cambridge, Mass., 1950, p. 126.

[3] E.g. *La Nonne . . .*, ll. 328–335: *Tresdoulce vierge debonnaire.*

fitted to such a setting. A major drawback is, however, that such pieces, in the mid and late fourteenth century at least, were normally sung by a soloist with instrumental accompaniment. Many of the Miracle *Rondeaux* do, indeed, display features of metre and versification more usually associated with the very early years of the fourteenth century, before the present Miracle cycle had begun. Maybe there had been earlier Miracle collections which have failed to survive; some of the *Rondeaux* in them could have been preserved and used again in the later collection. Some seem well-adapted to their particular context, but others do not fit especially well and a few examples are used in more than one play, separated by an interval of several years.[1]

In *La Nonne* . . . the three *Rondeaux* included are all on the simple eight-line pattern[2]:

Music: I   II   I   I   I   II   I   II
Text: A   B   a   A   a   b   A   B

Tresdoulce vierge debonnaire (ll. 328–335) and *Röyne de misericorde* (ll. 844–851) use the normal mid-fourteenth-century octosyllabic line; *Dame du royal empire* (ll. 426–433) uses the earlier seven-syllable line. Instead of introducing a further *Rondeau* for the final ascent to Heaven (ll. 884–887), the second half of *Röyne de misericorde* is repeated.

In *Saint Valentin* only two *Rondeaux* are used, but in each case the second half is repeated for the return journey to Heaven. *Venez vous en, benëurez* (ll. 1041–1048) is on the eight-line pattern, with octosyllabic lines. *Dame, par qui grace et merci* (ll. 330–342), similarly octosyllabic, is on the thirteen-line pattern seldom encountered after the early years in the secular fourteenth-century *Rondeau* repertory:

Music: I   II   I   I   I   II   I   II
Text: AB   B   ab   AB   ab   b   AB   B

5. STAGING

These plays were performed indoors, at the end of a hall, possibly on a slightly raised platform. The scenic principle of all mediaeval theatre is that of *décor simultané*: in other words, *all* the scenes which are

---

[1] See L. Müller, *Das Rondel in den französischen Mirakelspielen* . . . , Marburg, 1884, pp. 47–50.

[2] For full information on the lyric *formes fixes*, see N. Wilkins, *One Hundred Ballades, Rondeaux & Virelais* . . . , Cambridge, 1969.

involved in the action of a play are visible, side by side, throughout the entire performance; there is no question of 'scene-changing'. Each scene, or *mansion*, is a self-contained structure or blackcloth and they are arranged in a semi-circle with the *parloir*, or general acting area in front. It is a convention that Heaven and Hell, when represented, should stand on stage right and stage left respectively, the former on a raised platform, the latter in the gaping jaws of some fiendish beast. The present manuscript source, however, gives few specific instructions about the disposition of the *mansions* or the movements of the charac-ters.[1] We have to deduce these essential practical points from what we know of the few sources which do give stage directions and from external evidence such as narrative descriptions[2] and account books giving details of the expenses involved in the production of a play.[3]

On the basis of this background knowledge, we may suggest the following arrangements for our two plays:

La Nonne qui laissa son abbaie

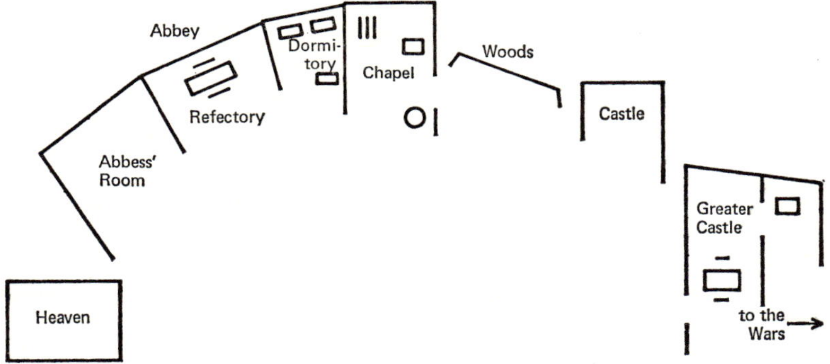

Heaven is a raised dais with steps leading up, probably decorated with flowers; a bench is needed for Notre Dame and the archangels, one seated on either side of her.

The Abbey is a complicated structure: the Chapel must have an outside door on the castle side and also a door leading into the rest of the building. There must be a pulpit with benches facing it, and a statue of the Virgin by the outside door. Windows could be painted or cut out. Three beds are needed in the dormitory, the bed of the second nun

---

[1] The only original stage direction in our chosen plays comes in *Saint Valentin*, preceding line 1125.

[2] E.g. Froissart's description of the pageantry which accompanied the entry of Queen Isabeau into Paris in August 1389.

[3] See especially G. Cohen, *Livre de Conduite du Régisseur . . .*, Paris, 1924.

preferably close to the door leading to the chapel. The refectory should be equipped with a table and bench. The abbess' room needs maybe a desk and a few chairs.

Between the Abbey and the Castle a backcloth or shrubs suggesting woods is needed, to emphasize the idea of journeying and to provide cover for the waiting knight and squire.

The first castle should be well equipped with hanging tapestries, chairs and other furniture.

The greater castle should be more sumptuously furnished, with a banqueting hall large enough for the minstrels' performance, and a bedroom.

Distance can be suggested by full use of the *parloir* area: for example, Notre Dame and the angels, when moving to the chapel, could process to far stage left before retracing their steps; similarly the final procession, singing *Veni Creator Spiritus*, could make a complete tour before exiting on stage right.

Saint Valentin

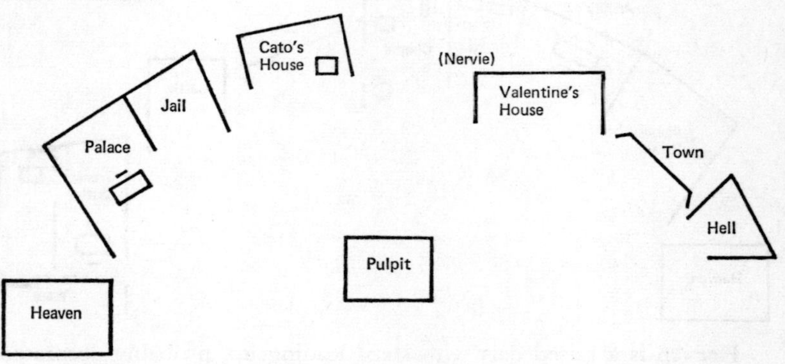

The opening sermon may be preached from a pulpit or slightly raised dais in stage centre. This could then be removed if it is an impediment.

Heaven and Hell follow the normal conventions. If it can be arranged to have smoke pouring out of the jaws of Hell, so much the better.

The Palace should convey the grandeur of imperial Rome and contain space and equipment for the Emperor's fatal banquet and for the torture and beheading of the prisoners. A jail is attached.

Cato's house must have a bed for his ailing son, and could be equipped with desks and books to suggest a centre of learning.

Valentine's house should be some way off, on the other side of the stage, and should be extremely simple, decorated by little apart from a crucifix. A backcloth could suggest the nearby town in which the students wander while awaiting Valentine's decision.

Again, the full stage space should be used, especially for the journey to and from Nervie, the sorties of devils, and the final angelic procession bearing Valentine's soul to heaven.

6. SOURCES AND INFLUENCE

As we have seen, the material used as a basis for the Miracles was adapted from varied sources, both religious and secular, mediaeval and ancient. The idea of giving dramatic form to a miracle was not entirely new: apart from Latin plays, the obvious thirteenth-century examples in the vernacular are Rutebeuf's *Le Miracle de Theophile* (a miracle of the Virgin) and Bodel's *Le Jeu de Saint Nicolas* (featuring the saint). The idea of including songs in a play was similarly no novelty. The liturgical drama from which the vernacular theatre grew was, of course, entirely 'music drama', sung from start to finish.[1] Adam de la Hale inserted many songs into his pastoral *Jeu de Robin et de Marion*, including a popular *Rondeau*.[2] The particular combination of songs with miracles of the Virgin, however, together with the basis of many of the miracle plots, seems unmistakably to be derived from the voluminous narrative *Miracles de Notre Dame* (c. 1214–33) by the churchman Gautier de Coinci (c. 1177–1236). The liturgical repertory of the church of St. Martial in Limoges, which holds a place of particular importance in the history of Church music, contains among its many *Versus* settings a number of *contrafacta*, in which Marian hymns replace texts on some other subject while retaining the original melody. Gautier de Coinci's originality seems to have been his adaptation of the courtly lyric forms of the troubadours and trouvères to make his own songs to the Virgin. The insertion of courtly lyrics into a narrative had been proudly initiated only a few years before (c. 1200) by Jean Renart, in his romance of *Guillaume de Dôle*.[3] Gautier de Coinci's lyrics in praise of Mary were equally the principal influence later on the polymath King Alfonso the Wise of Castile, in his *Cantigas de Santa Mariá* (thirteenth century). The *serventois* which follow many of our fourteenth-century Miracle plays, as well as the religious *Rondeaux* contained within them, owe a great deal to the early example. The use of interpolated *Rondeaux* was greatly exploited and elaborated in the fifteenth- and even sixteenth-century

[1] E.g. *The Play of Daniel*, ed. N. Greenberg, O.U.P., 1959.
[2] *Robins m'aime*.
[3] Ed. F. Lecoy, (CFMA) Paris, 1963.

French theatre. In addition, the Miracles de Nostre Dame as a whole, together with such isolated fourteenth-century examples as the *Passion du Palatinus*,[1] show clearly the line of development of religious drama towards the great fifteenth-century Passion cycles.

La Nonne qui laissa son abbaie is closely related to a miracle of Gautier de Coinci,[2] which is itself only one of six surviving versions from the thirteenth and early fourteenth centuries.[3]

Saint Valentin bears a certain similarity to an extant Latin life of the saint, though many details vary. It seems probable that our author had some further source which has failed to survive.[4]

7. THE MANUSCRIPT

The *Miracles de Nostre Dame* are contained in a unique late fourteenth-century manuscript now bound in two volumes contained in the Bibliothèque Nationale, Paris, fonds français 819–820. It is well preserved and neatly copied; each play is preceded by an attractive miniature depicting an important scene. The most striking paleographic feature, and one which has received much attention in recent years, is that the rubrics preceding each play contain certain erasures: in some cases substantial parts of the headings have been removed. It is through attempts to decipher these imperfect rubbings-out that it has emerged that the miracles belonged to the Goldsmith's Guild and that the plays were presented by them nearly every year. Originally each one of them was dated. An attractive and reasonable solution to the problem of why the erasures were made has been put forward by G. Runnalls[5]: he suggests that the manuscript was part of the sumptuous

[1] Ed. Grace Frank, (CFMA) Paris, 1922.

[2] Ed. V. Koenig, *Gautier de Coincy: Les Miracles de Nostre Dame*, 3 vols., (TLF) Geneva, 1955–66: Vol. III, pp. 191–213 "De la nonain qui quitta son abbaye".

[3] See H. Kjellman, "Le Miracle de la Sacristine", in *Mélanges de philologie offerts à M. J. Melander*, Upsala, 1943, pp. 47–81. Cf. also an item from *Las Cantigas de Santa Mariá* summarized in P. Dronke, *The Mediaeval Lyric*, London, 1968, pp. 71–72.

[4] See A. Jeanroy, in *Histoire littéraire de la France*, Vol. XXXIX, Paris, 1959, pp. 55–56.

[5] See "The Manuscript of the *Miracles de Nostre Dame par personnages*", in *Romance Philology*, Vol. XXII, No. 1 (1968), pp. 15–22 and "The *Miracles de Nostre Dame par personnages*: Erasures in the MS, and the Dates of the Plays and the 'Serventois' ", in *Philological Quarterly*, Vol. XLIX, No. 1 (January 1970), pp. 19–29.

gifts presented by the Guilds and eminent citizens to Queen Isabeau on her ceremonial entry into Paris in August 1389; the scribe would have copied in error information from the Goldsmiths' records of their meetings and at the last moment this would have been seen as inappropriate, since the gifts were to come from the 'bourgeois de Paris' in general rather than from any particular section of the community in isolation.

The later history of the manuscript is vague until its presentation to the Bibliothèque Royale in 1733, along with his whole private library, by the Duke Châtre de Cangé. Hence the frequent description of the collection as the 'manuscrit Cangé'.

8. SELECT BIBLIOGRAPHY

I. *General Works on the Mediaeval Theatre*

Albe, E., *La Confrérie de la Passion*, Paris, 1912.
Chambers, E., *The Mediaeval Stage*, 2 vols., Oxford, 1925.
Cohen, G., *Études d'histoire du Théâtre*, Paris, 1956.
Cohen, G., *La Mise-en-scène dans le théâtre religieux*, Paris, 1951.
Cohen, G., "Le Théâtre à Paris et aux environs au quatorzième siècle", in *Romania*, Vol. 38 (1909), pp. 587–595.
Cohen G., *Le Théâtre en France au Moyen Age*, 2 vols., Paris, 1928.
Frank. G., *The Medieval French Drama*, Oxford, 1954.
Jeanroy, A., "Le Théâtre religieux en langue française jusqu'à la fin du XIVe siècle", in *Histoire littéraire de la France*, Vol. XXXIX, Paris, 1959.
Leroy, O., *Études sur les mystères*, Paris, 1838.
Michel & Monmerqué, *Histoire du Théâtre en France au moyen âge*, Paris, 1839.
Roy, E., *Études sur le théâtre français du XIVe et du XVe siècle*, Paris, 1902.
Roy, E., *Le Mystère de la Passion en France du XIVe au XVIe siècle*, Paris, 1905.
Sepet, M., *Les origines catholiques du théâtre du moyen âge*, Paris, 1901.
Stratman, C., *Bibliography of Medieval Drama*, Berkeley & Los Angeles, 1954.
Stuart, D., *Stage decoration in medieval France*, New York, 1910.
Young, K., *The Drama of the medieval Church*, 2 vols., Oxford, 1933.

II. *Works on the Miracles de Nostre Dame par personnages*

Forkert, F., *Beiträge zu den Bildern aus dem altfranzösischen Volksleben auf Grund der "Miracles de Nostre Dame par personnages"*, Heidelberg thesis, 1901.
Frank, G., "The erasures in the Cangé MSS, 819, 820", in *Romance Philology*, Vol. XII (1958–59), pp. 240–243.
Glutz, R., *Les Miracles de Nostre Dame*, Berlin, 1954.

Jensen, H., *Die "Miracles de Nostre Dame par personnages" untersucht in ihrem Verhältnis zu Gautier de Coincy*, Heidelberg thesis, 1892.

Kelson, J., "The *Serventois* in the Cangé Manuscript", in *Philological Quarterly*, Vol. XLVII (1968), pp. 506–512.

Meyer, H., *Die Predigten in der "Miracles de Nostre Dame"*, Berlin, 1911.

Paris, G. & Robert, U., ed., *Les Miracles de Nostre Dame*, 8 vols., (SATF) Paris, 1876–83.

Penn, D., *The Staging of the "Miracles de Nostre Dame"*, New York, 1933.

Runnalls, G., *"Les Miracles de Nostre Dame par personnages": a Study of the Background and an edition of the fifteenth Miracle*, Exeter University thesis, 1966.

Stadler-Honegger, M., *Études sur "Les Miracles de Nostre Dame"*, Paris, 1926.

III. *Further Works for Reference*

Chailley, J., ed., *Les Chansons à la Vierge de Gautier de Coinci*, Paris, 1959.

Gripkey, M., *The Blessed Virgin Mary as Mediatrix in Latin and Old French Legend*, Washington, 1938.

Koenig, V., ed., *Gautier de Coinci: Les Miracles de Nostre Dame*, 3 vols., (TLF) Geneva, 1955–66.

Müller, L., *Das Rondel in den französischen Mirakelspielen und Mysterien des XV and XVI Jahrhunderts*, Marburg thesis, 1884.

*

I wish to express my gratitude to the British Academy, the Carnegie Trust for the Universities of Scotland and the University of St. Andrews, who made generous grants to aid my research and the publication of this edition.

N.W.

I

LA NONNE QUI LAISSA SON ABBAIE

Dramatis Personae

L'ABBESSE
PREMIERE NONNE (Prieure)
DEUXIESME NONNE
LE CHEVALIER
L'ESCUIER (Perrotin)
LE PRESCHEUR
NOSTRE DAME
GABRIEL
MICHIEL
LA DAMOISELLE
LE MESSAGIER
PREMIER FILZ
DEUXIESME FILZ

The second nun returns to the abbey
Paris, Bibliothèque Nationale, f.fr. 819
f. 69r°

MIRACLE
DE
LA NONNE QUI LAISSA SON ABBAIE

Cy commence un miracle de Nostre Dame d'une nonne qui laissa son abbaie pour s'en aler avec un chevalier qui l'espousa, et depuis qu'ilz orent eu de biaux enfans Nostre Dame s'apparut a elle, dont elle retourna en s'abbaie et le chevalier si rendi moinne.

(In the abbey dormitory)

<table>
<tr><td>L'ABBESSE</td><td>Mes suers, dites moy sanz sejour,
Il est hui grant feste et bon jour,
Avez vous point fait assavoir
Aux freres qu'un sermon avoir
Peussions hui?</td><td></td></tr>
<tr><td>LA PREMIERE
NONNE</td><td>Dame, se Dieu me gart d'annui,
G'y envoiay dès devant hier,
Et m'a mandé frere Gautier
Que sanz faillir icy venra;
Je ne say si me mentira
De sa promesse.</td><td>10</td></tr>
<tr><td>DEUXIESME NONNE</td><td>Nanil voir: espoir qu'il confesse,
Ou qu'il chante ou qu'il estudie;
Je ne doubt point, conment c'on die,
Que ci ne viengne.</td><td></td></tr>
</table>

(The nuns take their places in the chapel)

<table>
<tr><td>L'ABBESSE</td><td>Alons donc, aviengne qu'aviengne,
Noz places prendre et nous seons,
Et noz heures tout bas disons
En l'attendant.</td><td></td></tr>
<tr><td>PREMIERE NONNE</td><td>Dame, alons; j'ay le cuer tendant</td><td>20</td></tr>
</table>

> A faire vostre voulenté.
> Or sa, de par la Trinité,
> Seez vous ci.

L'ABBESSE C'est fait; or vous seez aussi
> Decoste moy.

DEUXIESME NONNE Dame, voulentiers; quant a moy,
> Je sui assise.

PREMIERE NONNE Et vezcy pour moy place prise.
> Je lo qu'ataingnons noz sautiers
> Et disons prime endementiers   30
> Que l'attendons.

L'ABBESSE C'est bien dit; a prier tendons
> Devotement.

(They pray, reading silently in their psalters. While the following scene is taking place the Preacher arrives at the abbey and makes his way across the chapel to the pulpit)

*   *   *

(Woods, near the abbey)

LE CHEVALIER Perrotin, vas sus, alons ment:
> Vers l'abbaie me fault traire,
> Car devers l'abbesse ay a faire,
> Qui est m'antin.

L'ESCUIER Sire, je croy miex pour certain
> Que l'amour de la nonne belle,
> Qui tant est sainte damoiselle,   40
> Laiens vous maine.

LE CHEVALIER Perrotin, c'est chose certaine;
> Certes, je l'ains tant que mon cuer
> Ne puis d'elle oster a nul fuer,
> Et si ne puis avoir sa grace
> Pour priere que je li face:
> Tu t'en peuz bien appercevoir.

                    Nonpourquant vueil j'aler savoir
                    Se je parler a lui pourray,
                    Ne se grace en lui trouveray   50
                         Qu'aie s'amour.

L'ESCUIER   Prest sui, sire; alons sanz demour
                    Ou vous plaira.

(They move towards the abbey)

LE CHEVALIER   Perrotin, par foy mal me va:
                    Vez la l'abbesse et la prieuse
                    Et la tresbelle gracieuse
                    Qui veulent oir le sermon.
                    Je vueil ci faire arrestoison
                         Pour l'escouter.

(The knight stops by the chapel doorway)

L'ESCUIER   Dont puis j'a l'ostel bien aler   60
                    Savoir qui vous demandera,
                    Et revenir quant vous plaira
                         Icy vous querre.

LE CHEVALIER   Tu diz verité; va bonne erre
                         Et reviens ja.

(The squire leaves for his master's castle)

                    *   *   *

(The sermon is preached from the pulpit)

LE PRESCHEUR
*Cum audisset, turbata est in sermone ejus, et cogitabat qualis esset ista
salutacio. Luce primo.*
     Doulce gent, au conmencement de nostre sermon nous
recourrons a la glorieuse vierge Marie, et lui prierons que elle
nous vueille donner grace a moy de dire et a vous de oir chose   [5]
qui soit a l'onneur de toute la court de paradis et a aucun
prouffit de noz ames et a la confusion de l'annemi. Et pour plus
briefment ceste grace empetrer, chascun et chascune, si vous
plaist, la saluera en disant: *Ave Maria.*

Cum audisset, turbata est in sermone ejus, et cogitabat qualis esset [10]
ista salutacio.

Doulce gent, il est de conmun cours que celles qui pour
l'amour de Dieu vivent en estat de virginité, a ce que elles soient
dites vraies vierges, que touzjours sont paoureuses et doubteuses,
et si que pour eschiver les choses qui sont a doubter elles [15]
craingnent a la foiz les choses seures; et qui fait ce? ce qu'elles
scevent qu'en un trop feible et fresle vaissiau, c'est assavoir en
leur corps qui ne sont que terre, elles portent un tresor precieux:
quoy? l'ame d'eulx, qui est faite a l'image de la benoite Trinité.
Et de ce avient que quant a telles vierges aucune chose vient de [20]
nouvel et soudainement, il machinent et souspeçonnent tantost
que ce ne soit contre eulz. Doulce gent, je le di pour tant que
quant Dieu li Peres ot envoié son ange a la glorieuse Vierge
Marie annoncier que elle seroit mere du fil de Dieu par qui la
redempcion de l'umain lignage seroit faite, a celle heure que li [25]
ange lui ot dit: "Dieu te saut, plaine de grace, Nostre Sires est
avecques toy", l'evangeliste saint Luc dit que la glorieuse Vierge
fu troublée et pensa quelle estoit ceste salutacion, et c'est la
sentence de la parole que je prononçay au conmencment de mon
sermon: [30]

Cum audisset, turbata est in sermone ejus, et cogitabat qualis esset
ista salutacio.

Conme la glorieuse Vierge eust oy le salut de l'ange, elle fut
troublée, ce dit l'evangeliste. Il ne dit pas partroublée, mais
troublée simplement, et ce vint de ce que elle estoit vierge [35]
vergondeuse et honteuse. Ce qu'elle ne fu pas partroublée fu de
la vertu de force qu'elle avoit en soy; ce qu'elle se tut et pensa
fu de la vertu de prudence. Elle pensa donc quelle estoit ceste
salutacion, dont il avint que quant li anges vit qu'elle pensoit, il
la conmença a conforter et a confermer ce dont elle doubtoit en [40]
disant: "Marie, ne te doubte pas, car en [ce] que je di n'a point de
de falace; n'y aies nule suspeçon; je ne suis pas homme, mais
esperit et ange de Dieu. Or ne doubtes donques point, car tu as
trouvé grace en Dieu. Ou se tu savoies combien ton humilité
plaist au treshault Dieu, tu ne jugeroies pas que tu ne soies bien [45]
digne de estre servie et de oir la parole des anges. Pourquoy te
diras tu non digne de la grace des anges, qui as trouvé grace a
Dieu, laquelle grace est la paix des hommes, la destruccion de
mort, la reparacion de vie? C'est dont grace que tu as trouvé a
Dieu, et en signe de ce vezcy que tu concevras et enfanteras un [50]
filz, qui sera appellé Jhesus."

Sur ce dit saint Bernart: O glorieuse Vierge, entens par le

nom du fil qui te est promis con grant et conme espicial grace
tu as trouvé a Dieu.

L'ange dit qu'il sera appellez Jhesus; la raison pour quoy   [55]
mett un autre evangeliste qui dit: *Ipse enim salvum faciet populum*
suum a peccatis eorum. Il sera appellez Jhesus; pour quoy? pour ce
que c'est celui qui sauvera son peuple de touz leurs pechiez.

Donques la glorieuse Vierge trouva bien grace a Dieu? Certes
voire, car elle est ou plus seur lieu de paradis par sa tresferme   [60]
foy; elle est ou plus hault par sa tresgrant humilité; elle est ou
plus pur par sa tresgrant chaasté et par sa nette virginité; elle est
ou plus glorieux par sa vraie purté, par sa vraie amour et par
l'excellence de sa grant charité. Du quel glorieux lieu elle fait
participans touz ceulx et toutes celles qui devotement en ce siecle [65]
la veulent servir et amer. Ou nombre desquelx nous vueille par
sa tresgrant misericorde acompaignier Dieu le Pere et le Filz et
le Saint Esperit, qui en Trinité regne et vit et regnera sanz fin.
Amen.

(The Preacher descends solemnly from the pulpit and leaves the chapel)

*   *   *

(Outside the chapel)

LE CHEVALIER De passion chiet cil en hen
       Par qui me sui ci tant tenuz!
       Egar! je fusse puis venuz
       Quatre liues qu'il ne fina.
       Je me merveil se grant mal n'a   70
        En sa cervelle.

(Within)

L'ABBESSE Ha! tresdoulce vierge pucelle,
       De pitié, de grace et d'amour,
       Moult fait en terre bon labour
       Qui vous aime, sert et honneure,
       Et cilz est nez de moult male heure
       Qui de cuer vous servir n'entent,
       Car a la perdicion tent
        De sa povre ame.

PREMIERE NONNE Certes, vous dites voir, ma dame,   80

Bon la fait servir et amer.
Car de doulceur est sanz amer
    La tresoriere.

L'ABBESSE   Et vous, ma doulce amie chiere,
Avez bien oy ce preudomme?
S'il estoit cardinal de Romme,
S'a il dit de belles raisons,
Benoist soit le jour q'un telz homs
    De femme naist.

DEUXIESME NONNE   Oil, ma dame: Diex li laist   90
Parfaire le bien qu'a empris;
Car d'amer Dieu est moult espris,
    Selon m'entente.

(The abbess turns to the first nun)

L'ABBESSE   Prieure, venez sanz attente
A moy en ma chambre parler,
Ainçoys qu'ailleurs pensez d'aler.
    Je vois devant.

PREMIERE NONNE   Dame, après vous m'en vois suivant
    Sanz plus ci estre.

(The abbess and the first nun leave the chapel, while the second nun kneels in prayer)

DEUXIESME NONNE   Et je me vois a genouz mettre   100
Devant l'image Nostre Dame
A qui j'ay donné corps et ame
A lui servir, et mon pensé.
Dame par qui fumes tensé
De la mort d'enfer pardurable
Quant Dieu le Pere esperitable
Fist son filz des haulx cieulx descendre
En vous et humanité prendre
Pour nous mener en paradis,
Dame qui en faiz et en dis   110
Plus qu'autre par prerogative
Futes a Dieu contemplative
[En] sainte conversacion,

Dame, toute m'afeccion,
Ma plaisance et tout mi desir
Sont en faire vostre plaisir.
Or m'en donnez, s'il vous plaist, grace,
Dame, et tandis que j'ay espace.
Voz heures cy recorderay
Et en disant accorderay   120
    La bouche au cuer.

(The knight watches the nun at prayer)

LE CHEVALIER   Certes, or ne say j'a nul fuer
Quelle contenance ait en moy,
Quant maintenant là endroit voy
Ce qu'ay desiré si long temps:
C'est ma dame noble et plaisans,
Courtoise, amoureuse et fetice.
Par le saint baron de Galice,
Se je devoie tout despendre
Quanque j'ay, si vouldray je tendre   130
A avoir s'amour maintenant.

(The knight enters the chapel)

E! tresgracieuse avenant,
Diex vous doint tresbonne aventure
Comme a ycelle creature
Qui plus est de mon cuer amée.
Or me soit vostre amour donnée,
    Tresdoulce amie.

DEUXIESME NONNE
  (Taken by surprise)

Sire, d'amer n'ay nulle envie
Fors que Dieu et sa doulce mere.
Certes, l'amour est trop amere   140
Dont ci endroit me requerez.
Ce n'est pas ce que vous querez,
    Sire, pour voir.

LE CHEVALIER   E! belle, plaine de savoir,
Vers vous ne vueil de riens mesprendre.
Plaise vous cest anel a prendre

> Que par fine amistié vous tens
> Et qu'avec vous hui mais seans
> Me puisse esbatre.

(The knight holds out a ring, which the nun brushes aside)

DEUXIESME NONNE   Folie vous feroit embatre   150
> Là ou l'en n'a cure de vous.
> Par foy, miex voudroie avoir roupz
> Touz les deux braz.

LE CHEVALIER   Cuer doulx, ne me refusez pas!
> Se vous faites ma voulenté,
> Je vous feray par verité
> Bien riche dame.

DEUXIESME NONNE   A Dieu me rens de corps et d'ame,
> Biau sire: laissiez moy en paiz.
> Je ne pris voz diz ne voz faiz,   160
> Si m'aist Diex, ce festu ci.
> Pour Dieu, alez vous ent de cy;
> Laissiez me ester!

(The knight leaves despondently)

LE CHEVALIER   Elas! bien me doy dementer:
> J'ay du tout failly a ma proye.
> A chose que ma bouche proie
> Ne veult celle que j'ains entendre.

(His squire approaches)

> Et dont viens tu? c'on te puist pendre!
> M'as tu bien fait icy muser?
> Sui je homme qui doye ruser   170
> Seul enmy voie?

L'ESCUIER   E! mon seigneur, que Dieu vous voie!
> Combien a que je sui venuz
> Et que je me sui ci tenuz
> Pour ce qu'a vous n'osoie aler?
> Je vous regardoie parler
> A celle dame.

LE CHEVALIER   Haro! c'est la plus dure fame
C'onques mais vi et la plus fiere.
Un seul tantait de belle chiere   180
Ne puis de lui traire n'avoir
Par priere ne pour avoir.
Briefment c'est le court et le lonc:
Autres femmes ont cuer de plonc,
Mais elle l'a de fer trop fort;
Quant je n'y puis trouver confort,
        Ne say que face.

L'ESCUIER   Sire, avant que de celle place
S'en voit arriere, a li alez
Et doulcement a li parlez;   190
Et se elle vous fait des refus
N'en soiez ja pour ce confus,
Mais s'amour touzjours requerez,
Et certainement vous l'arez
        Par ceste guise.

LE CHEVALIER   Tu m'as ci bonne voie apprise,
Perrotin; certes, g'y revois.
Or m'atens.

(*The knight returns to the chapel*)

                E! gent corps courtois
Pour cuer d'ami faire esjoir,
Vueillez vostre amant vray oir   200
        Qui se complaint.

DEUXIESME NONNE   Sire, de vous ay eu maint
Tel parler, dont petit me chaut:
Il ne me font ne froit ne chaut,
        N'en doubtez mie.

LE CHEVALIER   E! cuer doulx, [devenez] m'amie:
Humblement de cuer vous em proy,
Et je vous promet de ma foy
Quanqu'il vous plaira je feray,
Ne ja a riens ne contrediray   210
        Que vueillez dire.

DEUXIESME NONNE   Je n'aray mie paix, biau sire,
S'a vous amer ne me consens.
Ore pour ce que voi et sens
A voz maintiens que vous m'amez,
Et je ne vueil que diffamez
Soit mon corps par delit charnel,
Je vous fas ce jeu parti tel:
Je [sai] bien que nobles homs estes,
Et je de nobles gens honnestes   220
Sui estraitte aussi, qui sui femme.
Se pour miex garder de diffame
Mon honneur et mon pucellage
Vous me voulez par mariage
Prendre et le plevir par la foy,
Mon corps et m'amour vous ottroy;
    Autrement non.

LE CHEVALIER   Dame, pour vostre bon renom
Garder, et je le vous promet
De ma main qu'en la vostre met   230
    Trestoute nue.

DEUXIESME NONNE   Or n'en soit plus raison tenue
Quant a ore, ains vous en alez,
Et ja quant nuit sera venez
Et m'atendez en ce lieu là,
Et quant le convent dormira
Tout coiement m'en ysteray
Et a vous tout droit m'en venray:
    N'en doubtez mie.

LE CHEVALIER   C'est bien dit, belle doulce amie.   240
A Dieu dont vous conmanderay,
Et je vous y attenderay
    Certainement.

DEUXIESME NONNE   Je ne vous faudray nullement,
    N'en doubtez point.

(*The knight leaves joyfully*)

LE CHEVALIER   Certes, or me va bien a point:
J'ay trouvé en ma dame grace.

Qui me tenroit que ne chantasse?
Nulz, car j'ay le cuer plain de joie!

(*He sings*)   *Il n'est vivant qui me doie*   250
                      Blamer de celle servir
                      Dont tout bien me puet venir.

Venir? certes, voire a largesce
Quant seulement de sa promesse
          M'a fait si lié.

(*He rejoins his squire*)

L'ESCUIER   Mon seigneur, gay et esveillié
Vous voi plus que ne fis pieça.
Dites, s'il vous plaist, conment va
          Vostre besongne.

LE CHEVALIER   Bien, par la dame de Bouloingne!   260
Perrotin, j'ay quanque je vueil!
La belle qui tant a ver oeil
M'a fait present de son gent corps,
Et sommes en certains accors.
Alons men boire sanz delay.
Sachiez assez tost revenray
          Yci la querre.

L'ESCUIER   Or alons, mon seigneur, bonne erre,
          Qu'il est ja tart.

(*They depart for the castle. It grows dark*)

*   *   *

(*In the chapel*)

L'ABBESSE   Prieure, se Jhesus vous gart,   270
Trop me merveil de nostre suer
Conment peut durer a nul fuer
          Tant en l'eglise.

PREMIERE NONNE   Dame, elle est toute en Dieu esprise:
Touzjours est devant nostre dame.
Certes, c'est une sainte femme,
          A mon cuidier.

L'ABBESSE Prieure, ce n'est d'ui ne d'yer,
Mais dès lors que ceens entra.
Alez la faire venir ça, 280
S'irons couchier.

PREMIERE NONNE Voulentiers: je la vois huchier.

(She approaches the second nun)

Suer, l'abbesse vous mande ainsi
Qu'a li vous en venez de ci
Sanz demourée.

DEUXIESME NONNE Suer, je vois, puis qu'il li agrée:
Plus ne vueil ci faire demour.

(They rejoin the abbess)

Ma dame, Dieu vous doint s'amour
Par son plaisir.

L'ABBESSE Et il vous doint vostre plaisir. 290
Suer, il nous fault aler couchier:
Pensons d'en dortoir nous fichier;
Il est saisons.

PREMIERE NONNE C'est mon, car jours avons moult longs
Et courtes nuiz.

DEUXIESME NONNE Alons, dame, je vueil cest huis
Fermer, puis que sommes dedans,
Afin que nul ame ceens
Ne puist entrer.

(She closes the outer chapel door and they retire)

*   *   *

(The squire and the knight leave the castle)

LE CHEVALIER Perrotin, sanz nous plus monstrer, 300
Alons men là la belle attendre,

Car il m'est bien mestier d'entendre
Quant elle ystra.

L'ESCUIER Mon seigneur, ou il vous plaira
Tantost alons.

(In the dusk they travel to the abbey)

LE CHEVALIER Ho! Perrotin, ci nous tenons
Sanz dire mot chascun tout coy.
Seoir me vueil en ce recoy:
Siez toy aussi.

L'ESCUIER Sire, voulentiers: vez me cy   310
Lez vous assis.

(They sit down outside the chapel and wait in hiding)

*   *   *

(Heaven)

NOSTRE DAME Or sus, mi ange et mes amis,
Alons nous en celle abbaye.
G'i voy de pechier envaie
Une nonne que de cuer ainz:
Monstrer li vueil sa foleur ains
Qu'elle y enchiée.

GABRIEL Dame, alons; folz est qui ne bée
A faire vostre voulenté.
Or nous fault estre entalenté,   320
Michiel, de chanter, en alant
Devant no dame, aucun biau chant.
Il appartient.

MICHIEL Puis que chanter nous esconvient,
Gabriel, disons ce rondel
Qu'apris avons tout de nouvel,
Sanz [riens] retaire.

(Singing, they descend to the chapel; Notre Dame takes the place of her statue)

Rondel

Tresdoulce vierge debonnaire,
De vraie humilité sejour

Et d'amour parfaicte exemplaire,   330
Tresdoulce vierge debonnaire,

A tout cuer embelir et plaire
Doit qu'il vous serve nuit et jour,

Tresdoulce vierge debonnaire,
De vraie humilité sejour.

NOSTRE DAME   My ange, un petit de demour
Ici endroit nous trois ferons.
Assez briement nous en irons
            En paradis.

(The second nun steals out of the dormitory and enters the chapel)

DEUXIESME NONNE   Puis que convent est endormiz,   340
Il esconvient que je m'en aille:
Ce n'est pas raison que je faille
D'aler ou j'ay convenancié
Par grant amour et fiancé
Au doulx a qui le mien cuer tent,
Car trop annuie a qui atent,
Je le sçay bien, n'est pas nouvelle;
Mais avant par ceste chappelle,
Ou passer parmy me convient,
La doulce vierge par qui vient   350
Grace aux humains des cieulx ça jus
A mains jointes, a genouz nuz,
Humblement saluer m'en vois
De cuer devot a basse vois.

(She kneels before the Virgin)

Vierge, qui tant nous a valu
Contre Sathan, je vous salu
En disant: *Ave Maria,*
Gracia plena, dominus tecum, benedicta tu in
            mulieribus
Et benedictus fructus ventris tui.

(She stands up)

Dame, a Dieu! je m'en vois maishui: 360
Plus ne vous vueil ore aourer.

(The Virgin moves to bar the door)

Egar! me fault il demourer?
Mere Dieu, que peut ce ci estre?
Vostre ymage s'est venu mettre
Si droit au travers de cest huis
Que nullement passer ne puis.
E! doulx amis, vous muserez!
Vostre amie huimais pas n'arez,
Dont moult forment au cuer me poise.
C'est nient, il fault que m'en voise 370
        En [mon] dortoir.

(The nun returns to her dormitory)

*   *   *

(Outside the abbey)

LE CHEVALIER Haro! je croy que le povoir
De Dieu est du tout mis au nient
Quant celle que j'atens ne vient,
Ou je ne say s'elle me ruse
Pour moy faire paier la muse
        Ci toute nuit.

L'ESCUIER Vraiement, mon seigneur, je cuit
Qu'elle se soit de vous moquée:
Mienuit est ja plus que passée, 380
        Je vous promet.

LE CHEVALIER Voirement qui en femme met
Son cuer, bien le doit on blasmer,
Car on y treuve moult d'amer
Ainçois que l'en en viengne au bout.
Et, par Dieu, combien qu'il me coust,
Encore ci l'attenderay
Jusques a tant que je verray
        Le jour crevé.

(Dawn comes and the knight, disconsolate, returns to his castle. A day passes and at dusk he returns to take up again his hiding place outside the abbey)

* * *

(The next night; in the dormitory)

DEUXIESME NONNE   Que peut c'estre? Ay je sens desvé   390
        Ou j'ay esté enfantosmée,
        Qui ne puis estre oultre passée
        Celle chappelle ou ore entray?
        Par Dieu, encore me mettray
        En essai se pourray passer.

(She returns to the chapel)

        Pener me doy bien et lasser,
        Afin d'acomplir ma promesse,
        Car je seray chevaleresse
        Se de ceens puis estre yssue.
        Je m'en revois sanz attendue,   400
        Si saray qui m'en avenra.

(She kneels before the Virgin)

        Doulce Dame: *Ave Maria,*
        Gracia plena, dominus tecum, benedicta tu in
         mulieribus
        Et benedictus fructus ventris tui.

(She gets up. The Virgin again bars the door)

        Or doi j'avoir bien plain d'annui
        Le cuer, et de courrouz et d'ire,
        Quant ceste ymage contredire
        Deux foiz m'est venue a passer,
        Et je n'ay plus par ou aler
        Puisse, se n'est par ci endroit.
        Aussi con sur moy clamast droit   410
        L'issue par cy me devée;
        Je voy bien qu'en vain muse et bée:
        Retourner en dortoir me fault,

Mais le cuer de douleur me fault
Quant g'y revois.

(The nun returns to the dormitory)

*   *   *

NOSTRE DAME Ralons nous en entre nous trois,
Mi ange, en la gloire infinie,
Et si chantez a voiz serie
Aucun rondel.

(She puts the statue back in its place)

GABRIEL Nous en dirons un tout nouvel,   420
Dame, quant vous le conmandez.
Michiel, avecques moy chantez
Et sanz decort.

MICHIEL Disons donc ce rondel d'accort,
[Bel est a dire.]

(Singing, the angels escort Notre Dame back to heaven)

Rondel

Dame du royal empire
Des cieulz, mere au roy des roys,

Mains vous sert homs, plus empire,
Dame du royal empire,

Car par vous de Dieu s'espire   430
Grace ès cuers plains de desrois,

Dame du royal empire
Des cieulz, mere au roy des roys.

*   *   *

(Outside the abbey. Daybreak)

L'ESCUIER Mon seigneur, j'ay oy la vois
De l'aloete. Il est grant jour.
Alons men de cy sanz sejour,
C'on ne nous truisse.

« 31 »

LE CHEVALIER   Las! je ne say conment je puisse
Durer, tant ay au cuer courrouz.
Perrotin, va t'en, ami doulz,   440
Et revien assez tost a moy,
Car je te jur en bonne foy,
Jamais bien ayse ne seray
Tant qu'a elle parlé aray;
    N'en doubtes point.

L'ESCUIER   Je venray donc cy bien a point:
    Je m'en vois, sire.

(*The squire returns to the castle*)

*   *   *

(*In the dormitory*)

PREMIERE NONNE   Ma dame, encore avons a dire
Noz heures, et le jour est hault.
Trop avons dormy: il nous fault   450
    De ci lever.

L'ABBESSE   Hau! Diex, je prenoie a [resver].
Egardez conme il est haulte heure!
Or sus, alons men sanz demeure
    En cuer nous trois.

DEUXIESME NONNE   Ma chiere dame, alons, c'est droiz,
    Et temps en est.

(*The nuns get up and go into the chapel to pray*)

L'ABBESSE   A chascune son livre prest?
Je lo que tout bas versillons.
Mettons nous ci a genoillons
    En Dieu priant.   460

PREMIERE NONNE   Ce ne vueil j'estre detriant,
Ma chiere dame; or conmanciez:
Diner sera bien avanciez
    Ains qu'aions dit.

L'ABBESSE Conmencier vueil sanz contredit:
Domine, labia mea apperies.

LES SEURS *Et os meum annunciabit laudem tuam.*

L'ABBESSE *Deus, in adjutorium meum intende.*

LES SUERS *Domine, ad adjuvendum me festina.* 470

L'ABBESSE *Benedicamus Domino.*

LES SEURS *Deo gracias.*

(*They stand up*)

L'ABBESSE Alons diner ysnel le pas,
Puiz que noz heures dit avons,
Et après en dortoir yrons
    Sus la vesprée.

DEUXIESME NONNE Chiere dame, s'il vous agrée,
Un petit ici demourray,
Car encore un po a dire ay
    De mon service. 480

L'ABBESSE M'amie, je seroie nice
Se dire ne le vous laissoie.
Nous en irons par ceste voie
    Nous deux devant.

(*The first nun and the abbess go to the refectory.
The knight enters the chapel by the outside door*)

LE CHEVALIER E! doulce amie, en convenant
M'aviez d'estre a moy venue:
Par deuz nuiz vous ay attendue
Et a toutes deux musé ay,
Dont j'ay esté en grant esmay,
En grant courrouz et a malayse. 490
Pour Dieu, a moy dire vous playse
Qui m'a ce fait que ne venistes
Dès le convenant que me fistes
    Premiere foiz.

DEUXIESME NONNE Doulx sire, se conte de Foiz
 Feussiez, n'en peusse je faire
 Plus; ne vous vueille pas desplaire;
 Je l'amenderay bonnement,
 Car ennuit tout certainement
 Venray a vous entour mienuit, 500
 Sire, et pour Dieu ne vous ennuit
  De mon demour.

LE CHEVALIER Doulce amie, pour vostre amour
 Ne m'en vueil je pas courroucier,
 Mais je vous pri, dame, et requier
  Ennuit venez.

DEUXIESME NONNE Sire, pour tout certain tenez
 Que a vous vers mienuit iray:
 Pour nulle riens ne le lairay,
  Soiez en seur. 510

LE CHEVALIER Dame, [que] ce soit a bon eur.
 A Dieu! moult bien me prendray garde
 De vous, car moult forment me tarde
  Vostre venue.

(The knight returns to his castle)

DEUXIESME NONNE Bien sui fole quant tant tenue
 Me sui a servir ceste ymage
 Qui deux foiz m'a fait tel hontage
 Que le passer m'a deffendu
 Par cy, dont le cuer ay fondu
 Tout en douleur, c'est bien droiture. 520
 Mais pour nient prent ci de moy cure,
 Car de touz poins certes lairay
 Son service; plus n'en feray.
 Trop long temps en cloistre ay musé
 Et mon corps en penance usé:
 Plus n'en feray; j'en sui a fin.
 Ains qu'il soit demain au matin
 Pense j'estre en autre harnoys.
 Avecques l'abbesse m'en vois
  Qui m'atent là. 530

*   *   *

(The second nun joins the others in the refectory)

PREMIERE NONNE Bien veigniez, belle suer; or sa,
   Avez dit tout?

DEUXIESME NONNE Oil, j'ay tout mis sus le bout
   Jusqu'a demain.

L'ABBESSE C'est bien fait; mettez ci la main,
   Belle suer, avec nous mengiez.
   Tenez: ceste cuisse rungiez
   De ce poucin.

DEUXIESME NONNE Voulentiers, dame, de cuer fin
   Quant le voulez   540

(They dine)

PREMIERE NONNE Ma chiere dame, or m'entendez.
   Nous avons mengié a foison;
   Il est d'aler couchier saison,
   Si com me semble.

L'ABBESSE C'est voirs; alons nous trois ensemble.
   Demain lever nous convenra
   Matin, pour ce que l'en tenra
   Ceens chappitre.

DEUXIESME NONNE Alons donc: je ne vueil pas istre
   De vostre accort.   550

(The nuns return to the dormitory. Nightfall)

* * *

(In the castle)

LE CHEVALIER Perrotin, il m'est moult a fort
   De ce qu'estre autrement ne peut:
   Grant chose a en "faire l'esteut".
   Doulz amis, a toy me complaing.
   Je vieng de celle que tant aing,
   A qui j'ay parlé longuement

Et si li ay monstré conment
Deux nuiz elle m'a fait attendre;
Et elle d'umble cuer et tendre
M'a prié que je li pardoingne,   560
Car il li sourdi une essoine
Par quoy a moy ne pot venir,
Mais que ja venra sanz faillir;
    Que m'en diz tu?

L'ESCUIER   Mon seigneur, par le roy Jhesu,
Sachiez s'en vostre point estoie
Qu'a ceste foiz encore yroie
    Elle gaittier.

LE CHEVALIER   Pense donc de toy affaittier,
Car maintenant nous en yrons   570
Là endroit, et la gueterons
    Tant qu'elle viengne.

L'ESCUIER   Sire, ne dites plus qu'il tiengne
    A moy: prest sui.

LE CHEVALIER   Alons men, il est temps maishui,
    Tout bellement.

(The knight and his squire again set out for the abbey)

*   *   *

(The second nun creeps into the chapel)

DEUXIESME NONNE   Or ne vueil je plus longuement
Demourer que je ne m'en voise
De ci endroit sanz faire noise.
Convent dort, que je bien le say,   580
Et si me mettray en essay
De passer par my la chappelle
Sanz dire *ave*, ne kyrielle
Devant l'image de Marie;
Trop m'a fait estre en cuer marrie,
Dont plus saluer ne la vueil,
Ne tourner devers li mon oeil.
Dame, dame, tenez vous là.

Puis que passée suis de ça,
Je ne retourneray mais huy   590
Ne des mois, car je vois celuy
Que j'aim de cuer et que je quier
Qui m'atent là.

(She goes through the doorway unimpeded and joins the waiting knight)

Doulz ami chier,
A vous m'en vien.

LE CHEVALIER   Doulce amie, puis que vous tieng,
Je sui hors de toute tristesce
Et plain de joie et de leesce.
Vous soiez la tresbien venue,
N'y ait plus parole tenue;
Cy endroit plus ne demouron.   600
Or tost mettez ce chapperon
Et puis ce mantellet vestez.
Pour Dieu, dame, que vous hastez,
Car pour voir espouser vous vueil
Ains que je dorme mais de l'ueil;
N'en doubtez point.

(The nun puts on the coat and hat the knight has brought)

DEUXIESME NONNE   Sire, je suis preste et a point:
Avant mouvez.

LE CHEVALIER   Escuier, devant nous alez:
Passez tantost.   610

L'ESCUIER   Sire, voulentiers, a brief mot:
Je vois devant.

(With the squire leading, the couple journey to the castle)

*　　*　　*

(Next morning in the dormitory)

L'ABBESSE   Prieure, grant desavenant
Faisons de dormir à ceste heure.

> Levez sus tantost sanz demeure,
> S'alons chanter.

PREMIERE NONNE   Ma dame, je vois sanz tarder.
> Or sus, ma suer, sus sanz respit.

(The absence of the second nun is discovered)

> Egar! pas n'est dedanz son lit.
> Ou peut elle estre? 620

L'ABBESSE   Je ne say, par le roy celestre,
> S'elle n'est en l'eglise alée.
> Alons y voir sanz demourée
> S'elle y seroit.

PREMIERE NONNE   Dame, alons: de par Dieu ce soit;
> Il me plaist bien.

(They go into the chapel)

L'ABBESSE   Prieure, icy ne voy je rien.
> Je croy que ceens ne soit pas.
> Gardons partout ysnel le pas
> Pour l'amour Dieu. 630

(They look in every corner for the missing nun)

PREMIERE NONNE   J'ay gardé partout, mais en lieu
> De ceens ne la puis trouver.
> Je n'en say mais ou recouvrer
> Nouvelle vraie.

L'ABBESSE   Lasse! le cuer pour li m'esmaie.
> Aucuns hons si l'a deceue
> Pour ce qu'il l'a belle veue,
> Et ainsi l'en maine a diffame.
> Lasse! et c'estoit si sainte femme!
> Com grant damage! 640

PREMIERE NONNE   Voirement, plus a saint courage
> Une personne, et plus temptée
> Est du Sathan, afin qu'ostée

Soit de sa bonne voulenté.
Quel part qu'el voit, par sa bonté
    Dieu la deffende.

L'ABBESSE   *Amen*, m'amie, et la nous rende
Briement la doulce mere Dieu,
Qui mener la vueille en tel lieu
    Que mal ne face.   650

PREMIERE NONNE   Dame, sanz plus terme n'espace,
Je lo' qu'en vostre chambre entrons,
Et illecques regarderons
    Qu'en pourrons faire.

L'ABBESSE   Vous dites bien; c'est bon a faire.
    Prieure, alons.

(They go to the abbess' room)

*   *   *

(Several years pass.
In the castle)

LE CHEVALIER   Doulce amie, espousé avons
Et esté si lonc temps ensemble
Que deux enfans, si com me semble,
Avez de moy qui sont ja grans.   660
Nonpourquant sui bien recordans,
Je ne say se vous le savez,
Qu'encore demouré n'avez
Qu'en un de mes petiz hostieulx;
Mais je vous vueil mener ou mieulx
Que vous n'avez eu arez,
Et plus honnourée y serez
    Cent mile temps.

DEUXIESME NONNE   Mon treschier seigneur, je m'assens
A tout ce qui vous plaist a faire.   670
Se Dieu plaist, je ne quier meffaire
    Vers vous en rien.

LE CHEVALIER   Dame, de ce vous croy je bien;

Et je vous seray vraiz amis,
Si com je le vous ay promis,
    Jusqu'en la fin.

LA DAMOISELLE   Amer devez bien de cuer fin,
Ma dame, certes, mon seigneur.
Car il vous a fait le grengneur
Dame qui soit ici entour.   680
Jamais ne devez a nul tour
A sa voulenté contredire,
N'a chose qui lui plaise a dire
    Mettre encombrier.

DEUXIESME NONNE   Damoiselle, ne je ne quier,
    Par saint Martin.

LE CHEVALIER   Va t'en devant nous, Perrotin,
D'aprester l'ostel entremettre
Et de faire les tables mettre
    Pour le diner.   690

L'ESCUIER   Mon seigneur, je ne quier finer
S'aray fait, je vous convenant,
Vostre vouloir: je vois devant
    Tout aprester.

(The squire travels ahead to prepare for his master's arrival at a larger castle)

LE CHEVALIER   Dame, alons men sanz arrester
    Par ci aval.

[DEUXIESME NONNE]   Alons, que Dieu vous gart de mal,
    Mon chier seigneur.

LA DAMOISELLE   Dieu vous ottroit paix et honneur
Ensemble et longue et bonne vie,   700
Et deffende de male envie
    Par sa doulceur.

(The knight, his lady and the maidservant make the same journey)

*   *   *

(*The larger castle*)

LE CHEVALIER M'amie, vezci la meilleur
Maison que j'aie, sanz mentir.
Entrez ens; bien puissez venir:
Que Dieu le vueille!

(*They enter in*)

DEUXIESME NONNE Sire, Dieux a honneur recueille
Ès cieulx vostre ame!

L'ESCUIER Or tost a table alez, ma dame,
Et vous, mon seigneur: temps en est. 710
Je vous serviray; tout est prest,
Moult grant piece a.

(*The knight and his lady take their places at table*)

LE CHEVALIER Dame, vous serrez par dela
Et j'emprès vous.

DEUXIESME NONNE Voulentiers, mon chier seigneur doulz,
Quant vous aggrée.

(*The maid helps the squire to serve the meal*)

LA DAMOISELLE Et vez me ci toute aprestée
D'aidier a faire le service,
Car de ce ne suis je pas nice
Ny esgarée. 720

LE CHEVALIER Or tost, met cy sanz demourée,
Perrotin, se [mengier] devons,
De telz biens con ceens avons:
Delivre toy.

L'ESCUIER Voulentiers, mon seigneur, par foy:
Tenez, chier sire.

(*The squire brings food in dishes*)

(*Some minstrels come into the banqueting hall*)

LE CHEVALIER   Or me vas a ces jeugleurs dire
Qu'ilz viengnent ci sanz demourée.
Je vueil que soiez honnorée,
     Dame, seyens.   730

L'ESCUIER   Je vois. Seigneurs, venez leyens
     Faire mestier.

(The squire summons the minstrels and they perform songs and dances; a messenger interrupts the entertainment)

LE MESSAGIER   Diex gart de mal et d'encombrier
Ma dame et mon seigneur aussi
Et toute la gent autressy
     Que ceens voy.

LE CHEVALIER   Messagier, bien veigniez, par foy.
     Quelles nouvelles?

LE MESSAGIER   Sire, ilz ne sont mie trop belles.
Le conte de qui vous tenez   740
Vous mande ainsi qu'a li venez
Sus quanque vous pouez meffaire,
Car il a moult de vous affaire.
Plus ci endroit ne vous tenez,
Mais faites, si vous en venez,
Sire, a lui tost sanz demourée;
Car le prince de la Mourée,
Sire, l'est venu assaillir,
Et il se doubte de faillir
A soy contre lui revengier.   750
Il voit ja les bestes mengier
A ses gens, s'en a grant deffault;
Avec ce touz les jours assault
A grans et a petiz moult fort,
Si que s'il n'a briement confort
De vous et de ses autres gens,
Et que chascun soit diligens
A son pouoir de li aidier,
Je doubt bien, sire, que vuidier
Sa terre ne li esconviengne,   760
Et que le prince ne la tiengne
Comme seue acquise en sa main;

Si que, pour Dieu, et soir et main
Vueillez penser de chevauchier
Tant qu'a li soiez, sire chier.
Autre chose ne vous diray
Fors qu'a Dieu vous conmenderay.
Tout ce pais m'en vois cerchier
Et a touz ses hommes chargier
Autel conme je vous ay dit,   770
Et qu'il n'y facent contredit.
Pour Dieu, mettez vous tost a voie!
Vezci lettres qu'il vous envoie;
     Lisez les, sire.

LE CHEVALIER   Maintenant les me verras lire.

(The knight takes the letters from the messenger and examines them carefully)

Je voi assez son mandement.
Dame, sanz plus delaiement
Faire, au conte m'en fault aler
Mon seigneur, sanz plus demourer.
     A Dieu vous di.   780

DEUXIESME NONNE   Mon seigneur, alez a celi
Dieu qui vous fist, qui vous conduie
Et qui briement vous raconduie
     Sain et haittié.

LA DAMOISELLE   Dieu vous vueille par sa pitié,
Mon seigneur, en tel lieu mener
Que riens ne vous puisse grever,
Mais par tout là ou vous irez
Soiez des dames honnourez.
Je pri Dieu qu'il li en souviengne   790
Et qu'en santé il vous maintiengne
     Par son plaisir.

(The knight sets out to aid his overlord in war)

*   *   *

(Ten years pass.
The knight returns from the wars, accompanied by his squire)

LE CHEVALIER Dame, Diex yst, si grant desir
      N'[oi], je croy, passé a dix ans,
      Com de vous estre cy veans,
       M'amie chiere.

DEUXIESME NONNE Et j'ay vostre venue chiere
      Sur toute riens, mon seigneur doulx.
      Pour Dieu, conment le faites vous?
       Que bien veigniez!   800

(Scene of happy reunion)

LE CHEVALIER Dame, je suis sains et haitiez,
      Et conment le font noz enfans?
      J'ay esté lonc temps desirans
       D'estre avec eulz.

DEUXIESME NONNE Bien, sire; enfans, alez touz deux
      A genouz devant vostre pere;
      Saluez le de haulte chiere;
       Delivrez vous!

(The children run to greet their father)

[PREMIER FILZ] Mon frere, or sus, delivrons nous
      De no pere aler saluer: 810
      Ce ne nous doit en riens grever,
      Je sçay bien qu'aussi lui plaira.
      Mon seigneur, vous soiez deça
       Le bien venuz!

(Further scenes of joyful reunion)

LE CHEVALIER C'est assez, mes enfans, or suz.
      Dame, de chevauchier me dueil
      Trop malement; sachiez je vueil
       Aler couchier.

(The knight retires to bed)

DEUXIESME NONNE De par Dieu soit, mon seigneur chier;
      Le lit est tout prest, Dieu mercy. 820
      Escuier, sanz plus estre cy,

Prenez en l'estable un cheval
Et s'alez au giste a Loncval;
Vous avez assez heure et temps;
Et demain reçoif le chier cens
  C'on vous doit.

L'ESCUIER Ma dame, g'y vois bon esploit,
  Quant le voulez.

(The squire goes to find his lodging)

EUXIESME NONNE Damoiselle, et vous en alez
Sanz noise, et je couchier m'en vois 830
Delez mon seigneur; il est droiz.

(The maid retires. The lady finds her husband asleep and lies down beside him)

Qu'est ce là, mon seigneur? veilliez?
Il pert bien qu'il est traveilliez
  Quant ja se sort.
  * * *

(Heaven)

NOSTRE DAME Venez avec moy par deport,
My ange, car je vueil aler
Une moie amie appeller
De l'estat de pechié a grace.
Trop s'i est enlacie et lace.
  Alons briefment. 840

GABRIEL A vostre doulx conmandement,
Dame des cieulx, obeirons,
Et devant vous chantant yrons:
  C'est bien droiture.

MICHIEL Mouvons devant bonne aleure,
Gabriel amis, et chantons
Ce rondel cy que nous savons
  Bien sanz discorde.

(Singing, the angels escort Notre Dame to where the sleeping couple lie)

Rondel

Roÿne de misericorde,
Quant vostre grace a touz offrez,   850

Homs qui vostre doulceur recorde,
Roÿne de misericorde,

Sent qu'a Dieu par vous se racorde
Et que nul perir ne souffrez,

Roÿne de misericorde,
Quant vostre grace a touz offrez.

NOSTRE DAME Or sus, or sus de pechiez orde,
Or sus, or sus ysnellement!
Trop as mespris vilainement,
Qui si longuement m'as laissié   860
Pour un homme a qui adrecié
As t'amour et ton cuer du tout,
Qui te sera de trop chier coust
Si bien tost tu ne t'i prens garde.
Or sus, fole, plus ne te tarde,
Mes saluz tantost me rapportes,
Ou du ciel te clorray les portes!
L'anemi t'a bien decëu,
Quant en pechié as tant gëu.
Vien, si me sers con tu seulz faire,   870
Ou trop mal ira ton affaire,
Je te promet, en brief tempoire!

Ralons nous ent, my ange, en gloire,
Car je le vueil.

GABRIEL Dame, vostre conmant recueil
A faire en gré. Michiel amis,
Puis qu'a voye nous sommes mis,
Chantons, c'est droiz.

MICHIEL Je m'y accors en touz endroiz.
Vueillons nostre rondel pardire,   880
Gabriel, en alant sanz ire.
Faisons que l'un a l'autre accorde.

(Singing, the angels escort Notre Dame back to heaven)

Rondel

... Sent qu'a Dieu par vous se racorde
Et que nul perir ne souffrez,

Roÿne de misericorde,
Quant vostre grace a touz offrez.

*   *   *

(The couple wake up)

DEUXIESME NONNE   Lasse! bien doit estre effraez
Mon las de cuer, quant j'ay meffait
Contre Dieu si vilain meffait
Que de s'amour m'ame descorde.   890
E! dame de misericorde,
A la mort d'enfer vois le cours
Se ne me prenez en secours,
  Vierge Marie.

LE CHEVALIER   Qu'est ce là, ma tresdoulce amie?
Qu'avez vous qui cy lamentez
Et qui si fort vous dementez
  A vous meismes?

DEUXIESME NONNE   Ha! sire, le doulx roy haultismes
Me het, et il a bien raison,   900
Car male et mortelle traison
Ly ay fait pour la vostre amour.
S'en cest etat fas plus demour,
  Je suis perdue.

LE CHEVALIER   Egar! conme estes esperdue,
Belle dame! ou mains dites moy
Que vous avez, je vous em proy.
Il a bien trente ans, ce me semble,
Que nous assemblames ensemble;
Onques mais je ne vous vi mettre   910
En tel meschief con vous voi estre,
  N'en tel tristece.

DEUXIESME NONNE   Vous souvient il de la promesse
Que vous fis pieça, sire doulx,

      Quant premier deu venir a vous?
        Dites moy voir.

LE CHEVALIER   Oil, dame, par estouvoir,
      Et que je musay par deux nuiz
      Pour vous: ce me fu grant ennuiz
        Certainement.   920

DEUXIESME NONNE   Dès lors ouvray je folement,
      Mon seigneur, certes, ne doubtez;
      Vezci pour quoy. Or m'escoutez.
      Ces deux nuiz, con je vous avoie
      Convenant, je me mis a voie
      De venir a vous, biau doulx sire,
      Mais la mere Dieu contredire
      Me vint ces deux jours le passage
      Pour ce que j'avoie en usage
      De lui saluer humblement,   930
      Et l'avoie fait longuement.
      Dont quant je cuiday la chappelle
      Passer, l'ymage a la pucelle
      Trouvay de l'autel descendue
      Et encontre l'uis estendue;
      Lors contre lui me courrouçay,
      Qu'a la tierce nuit ne daignay
      Au passer saluer la dame;
      Et nonpourquant pour sauver m'ame
      Se part de cy, se m'a semblé;   940
      A cuer de courrouz enflambé
      M'a dit que se tost sanz demour
      Ne laisse la mondaine amour
      Et que d'elle servir me paine,
      Jugié sui a le grief paine
        D'enfer sanz fin.

LE CHEVALIER   Elle vous aime de cuer fin,
      Dame, a ce que je puis veoir.
      Par amour or me dites voir
        Que vouldrez faire.   950

DEUXIESME NONNE   Mon treschier seigneur debonnaire,
      Par aage avons bien passé nonne:
      Pour Dieu, que je ressoie nonne;

Car desoresmais vueil beter
Mon corps par penance et mater
Si que, se Dieu plaist, j'aquerray
L'amour de Dieu que perdu ay
    Par ma folie.

LE CHEVALIER   Dame, grant dueil en moy s'alie
Quant ainsi laissier me voulez;   960
Et nonpourquant vous le ferez,
Car a l'abbesse vous menray,
Qui est m'antain, et vous feray
Vostre paiz, ne vous doubtez mie.
Mais je vous dy bien, doulce amie,
Pour ce que pour m'amour yssistes
De cloistre et avec moy venistes,
Cloistrier pour vostre amour seray
Si tost qu'apaisié vous aray:
    Telle est m'entente.   970

DEUXIESME NONNE   Sanz plus faire cy longue attente,
Sire, pour Dieu, alons bonne erre
A l'abbesse mercy requerre.

(She looks at her sleeping children)

A ces enfans bien revenrez
Et, s'il vous plaist, vous leur ferez
    Bien, conme aux vostres.

LE CHEVALIER   Dame, je sçay bien qu'ilz sont nostres.
En la garde Dieu les lairay,
Car ja mais ne retourneray
Cy endroit pour biens que g'y aie.   980
La paour de Dieu trop m'esmaie,
Que griefment m'ame ne pugnisse
Pour les pechiez qu'ay faiz con nice.
Alons men tost, mouvez devant.
Mi enfant, a Dieu vous conmant
    Qui vous soit pere.

(The couple set out for the abbey)

*   *   *

(The children wake up and miss their parents)

PREMIER FILZ   Venez ça, ma dame ma mere.
Ma dame! Egar! respondez moy!
Ou est elle? pas ne la voy,
Ne mon pere. Ou sont il alé?   990
Je croy qu'ilz nous ont cy laissé.
Je me vueil lever; si saray
Se ceens trouver les pourray.
Egar! Je ne les treuve mie.
Haro! doulce vierge Marie,
    Ou est ma mere?

DEUXIESME FILZ   Qu'as tu, mon frere? Est ce mon pere
    Qui t'a batu?

PREMIER FILZ   Nanil, mais nous avons perdu
Ma mere; je te le promet: 1000
Je ne puis savoir ou elle est,
Ne mon pere ceens n'est pas.
Helas! ma dame, helas! helas!
    Que ferons nous?

DEUXIESME FILZ   Helas! ma dame, ou estes vous?
Ma dame, venez a nous ça.
Egar! elle n'est mie là.
    Helas! ma dame!

PREMIER FILZ   Or te tais, mon frere, et par m'ame
Je te donrray ja une noiz.   1010
Las! encore po me congoiz
Pour nous deux savoir gouverner,
Ne conment me doy demener,
    N'en quel affaire.

(The squire arrives)

L'ESCUIER   Enfans, qu'avez a ainsi braire
    Entre vous deux?

PREMIER FILZ   Escuier, nous sommes touz seulz
Laissié ceens conme esperdu,
Car pere et mere avons perdu,
    Si com me semble.   1020

(*The squire quickly masters his astonishment and takes charge of the
situation*)

<table>
<tr><td>L'ESCUIER</td><td>Je vous menray touz deux ensemble
Chiez vostre oncle. Y voulez venir?
De plourer vous faulra tenir
    Se vous y maine.</td><td></td></tr>
<tr><td>DEUXIESME FILZ</td><td>Quant g'i alay, l'autre sepmaine,
Il me donnit de son blanc pain
Et des pommes dedanz mon sain,
    Se m'aist Diex.</td><td></td></tr>
<tr><td>L'ESCUIER</td><td>Tu diz voir. Or torche tes yex;
Encore t'en donrra il ja.
Ne plourez plus vous deux; or ça!
Avecques moy vous en venez.
Espoir que vous y trouverez
Vostre mere qui s'y desjune,
Qui alée y est pour aucune
    Besongne faire.</td><td>1030</td></tr>
</table>

(*The squire and the two children leave the stage*)

*   *   *

(*In the chapel*)

<table>
<tr><td>LE CHEVALIER</td><td>Belle seur, bien va nostre affaire.
Se Dieu plaist, je voy là l'abbesse
Et avec lui la prieuresse:
Alons a genouz devant lui.</td><td>1040</td></tr>
</table>

(*The couple kneel before the abbess*)

Chiere dame, je sui celui
Qui requier [estre] a merci pris
De ce que j'ay vers vous mespris.
Car de ceens fortrais la nonne
Que vous teniez a tant bonne,
Et li ay fait rompre son veu.
D'estre nommé vostre nepveu
Ne sui mais digne, bien le say,
Pour le grant pechié que fait ay;

Nonpourquant je la vous ramaine, 1050
Et vous requier, pour la haultaine
Amour [qu'a] nous monstra li roys
Des cieulx quant voult morir en croiz,
Qu'elle a mercy soit receue
Et des draps de ceens vestue
Aussi qu'autre foiz a esté;
Et je vous jure en verité
Que se la voulez recevoir
Je devenray moine pour voir
    Sanz demourée. 1060

DEUXIESME NONNE   Conme honteuse et esgarée,
Ma dame, merci vous requier
Et desoresmais je ne quier
A vivre que d'yaue et de pain;
C'est droiz, car onques mais nonnain
    Ne meffist tant.

(*Pause*)

PREMIERE NONNE
(*To the abbess*)   Dame, soiez leur respondant
Aucune chose; mot ne dites!
Ce meffait leur soit clamez quittes,
    S'il vous agrée. 1070

L'ABBESSE   Il me font si estre esplourée
Que le cuer en lermes me font,
Pour la grant pitié qu'il me font,
Combien qu'a Dieu ont trop forfait.
Niez, puis que de vostre meffait
Vous repentez, et vous, m'amie,
Je ne vous refuseray mie
Pardon que vous me demandez,
Mais que voz viez amendez
Et que vous chastiez voz corps; 1080
Car Diex est plus misericors
Que pechier ne pouons d'assez.
Or pensez qu'en vous amassez
Planté de vertuz par bonne euvre,
Cat il ne fault pas qui recuevre,
    N'en doubtez, non.

LE CHEVALIER Ma belle ante, ce ne fait mon;
Et pour ce que g'y puisse entendre,
Je me vois moine cloistrier rendre.
A Dieu vous dy.   1090

(*A poignant moment; the couple exchange their last fond look. The knight
then swiftly leaves the stage, the nun fighting hard not to reach out after him*)

PREMIERE NONNE Dame, certainement vezci
Euvre de Dieu. Il y pert bien,
Quant tout son avoir terrien
Veult delaissier ce chevalier
Pour devenir moine cloistrier
Et pour bien faire.

L'ABBESSE C'est voirs, m'amie debonnaire,
Car il a esté trop mondains;
Et si ne prise je pas mains
De notre suer la repentance,   1100
Si que pour loer la puissance
De Dieu de cy nous en irons
Ou de nouvel la vestirons
De notre habit, c'est bien droiture;
Et en alant mettrons no cure
De bien chanter pour ces vertuz:
Veni, creator spiritus.

(*All three rise and leave the chapel in procession; their singing is joined by
the angels in heaven and by the minstrels. It rises to a triumphant climax as
they leave the stage*)

* * *

EXPLICIT

II

SAINT VALENTIN

Dramatis Personae

VALENTIN
L'EMPEREUR
PREMIER SERGENT
DEUXIESME SERGENT
CHATON
LE FILZ DE L'EMPEREUR
LE CHEVALIER
LE FILZ CHATON
JOSIAS, PREMIER ESCOLIER
DORECH, SECOND ESCOLIER
JOSEPHUS, TIERS ESCOLIER
BUZI, QUART ESCOLIER
LE QUINT ESCOLIER
LE NERVIEN
DIEU
NOSTRE DAME
GABRIEL
MICHIEL
VUIDEBOURSE, JOLIER
PREMIER DIABLE
DEUXIESME DIABLE
[LE PRESCHEUR]

Saint Valentine beheaded
Paris, Bibliothèque Nationale, f.fr. 820
f. 28r°

MIRACLE
DE
SAINT VALENTIN

(The sermon is preached from a pulpit, stage right)
[LE PRESCHEUR]

Frater qui adjuvatur a fratre quasi civitas firma. Proverbiorum XVIII°.
Ceste parole proposée en latin veult ainsi dire en françois: Frere
qui est aidié de frere est conme une cité bien fermée; et peut
estre exposé a nostre edifficacion, et y peuent estre notées trois
choses: permierement que nous sommes freres; secondement que
nous devons l'un l'auter aidier, qui est noté ici: *Frater qui
adjuvatur a fratre* – conme vous soiez freres, vous devez l'un
l'autre aidier; tiercement le proufit que nous y avons, se nous nous
entreaidons. Car nous serons si fors c'om ne nous pourra
vaincre. Et c'est touchié en ce qui dit: *quasi civitas firma.* Or   [10]
veons du premier. Vous devez savoir que par grace nous sommes
freres et germains. Pour quoy? Car nous sommes touz creez d'un pere,
c'est assavoir de Dieu, et d'une mere, c'est assavoir de sainte
eglise. Je ne di pas que nous soions ci assemblés conme con-
freres ne par maniere de confrarie, mais conme germains et freres
par amour et dileccion espirituelle. Dont nous nous devons plus
amer que freres charnelx, et je le te preuve, car, si conme dit
saint Ambroise, grace est plus contraignant a amer que nature,
car la mort separe et dessevre les choses jointes par nature, mais
elle ne peut separer les jointes par grace et par amour, car ainsi   [20]
fort est l'amour conme mort; avec ce vous savez que l'un frere
charnel appetice et amenuise l'eritage de l'autre frere, et de tant
conme ilz sont plus de freres charnelx de tant a chascun mendre
heritage: ce veons nous en la succession des peres et des meres;
mais le frere espirituel n'amenuise pas l'eritage de son frere
[espirituel], ainçois l'acroist, et cest heritage c'est vie pardurable.
Saint Augustin dit: Beneuré est l'eritage qui pour habondance
de hoirs n'apetice point, mais acroist, et cest heritage c'est vie
pardurable, et vie pardurable c'est congnoistre Dieu et li amer.
Vous veez que la mere qui voit que son filz est congneu et amé   [30]

de moult de gens, pour ce ne l'aime pas mains, mais plus, et
ainsi est il et sera en gloire lassus; car de tant com nous verrons
plus de noz freres amer Dieu, tant plus amerons nous Dieu. Car
aussi [conme] les freres, tant conme ilz sont en la mainburnie du
pere, toutes choses leur sont conmunes et s'entreaiment plus que
quant ilz sont divisez et separez, aussi nous estant espirituelment
en la mainburnie de Dieu, nous ne serons point divisez; et ainsi
le dit David, qui dit: Nostre seigneur me gouverne et je n'ay
deffaulte de rien. Et ou Fait des Appostres est il dit de la multitude des creans: C'estoit un cuer et une ame. [40]

Et pour ce doivent avoir grant honte et grant confusion
ceulx qui s'enorgueillissent de leur parentage et se vantent de
leur lignage de char et despisent les autres; et puis que nous
sommes freres germains, l'un n'a loy de despiter l'autre, ne
vituperer. Pour ce dit saint Augustin que touz hommes sont a
amer egalment, car nous sommes touz filz de Dieu, et ainsi le dit
le sauveur Jhesu Crist, *Mathei XXIII°*: *Patrem nolite, etc.*: Ne
dites que vous arez point de pere sur terre, non; car un est qui
est vostre pere, lequel est ès cieulx. Et Malachie le prophete dit:
Pour quoy despit un chascun de vous son frere, et n'est il qu'un [50]
pere de vous touz? Donques il n'y a point de difference entre
nous que nous ne soions touz freres au mains de la partie de
l'ame. Car elle n'est [creée] mais que de Dieu simplement. Et
puis que nous sommes freres, nous nous devons entreaidier, car
l'en dit que deux ou trois freres valent plus en une bataille que
cinc ou six estranges. Et pour Dieu avons nous point de bataille
a faire pour quoy nous doions l'un l'autre aidier? Certes oil, et
non pas pour une heure, mais tant conme nous sommes en ceste
mortel vie. Et ainsi le tesmoingne Job qui dit: Vie d'omme sur
terre ce n'est mais que une chevalerie. A qui avons nous la [60]
bataille? A qui? non pas au monde seulement, mais a la char et
a l'anemi. Pour quoy nous enorte saint Pol et nous prie: Mes
freres, je vous prie, vestez vous de l'armeure de Dieu, a ce que
vous puissiez resister et ester contre les agaiz de l'anemi. "De
l'armeure de Dieu" – c'est a dire que tu aies force en pacience et
biauté de continence a l'exemplaire de la glorieuse vierge mere
Marie, pour qui honneur et reverence nous sommes ci assemblez,
qui plus parfaictement entre les creatures de ce monde ot ces
vertuz en elle, c'est a dire force en pacience et biauté de continence. En la passion du benoit Jhesu elle ot la vesteure de force, [70]
car la douleur que Jhesu souffri de fait elle senti en soy par com-
passion, et ainsi l'avoit prophetisé le juste Simeon, quant il dist:
Et tuam ipsius animam pertransibit gladius – Marie, le glaive de la

passion de cestui (c'est de Jhesus) trespersera ton ame. Apres
elle ot biauté de continence, qui est une biauté sainte desirée
de Dieu, si conme David dit: *Cumcupiscet rex decorem tuum* – le
roy desire veoir ta biauté. "Le roy" – quel roy? celui qui donne
le bougueran de continence, la pourpre de pacience, le pers de
penitence, le vert d'abstinence, l'escarlate de martire, et le vair
d'onnesté, c'est l'amoureux Jhesus. Et pour ce se tu as ces deux   [80]
choses, force en patience et biauté de continence, tu seras vestu
et vestue de double vesteure, car pour ta pacience, tu aras veste-
ment de pourpre, pour ta continence vesteure de bougueran.
Apres tu aras pour ta [pacience] couronne de roses, pour ta continence couronne de lis. Et ainsi seras souffisanment acrue et
aournée, pour entrer aux noces de l'aignel Jhesu Crist, c'est a
dire en la gloire pardurable des cieulx, laquelle nous octroit *ille
qui est benedictus in secula seculorum. Amen.*

*   *   *

*Cy conmence un miracle de saint Valentin, que un empereur fist decoler devant
sa table, et tantost s'estrangla l'empereur d'un os qui lui traversa la gorge, et
dyables l'emporterent.*

(*The Emperor's Palace*)

L'EMPEREUR   Biaux seigneurs!

LES SERGENS   Que vous plaist, chier sire?

L'EMPEREUR   Alez m'au sage Chaton dire
      Sanz delay que je le demande,
      Et que pour cause je li mande
       Qu'il viengne ci.

PREMIER SERGENT   Il li sera dit tout ainsi,
      Sire, com vous le conmandez,
      Et qu'en haste le demandez.
       Alons le querre.

DEUXIESME   Alons, prenons par ci nostre erre: 10
 SERGENT   C'est, ce m'est avis, le plus court.

(*The sergeants go to Cato's house*)

Je le voy là en my sa court,
C'est bien a point.

PREMIER SERGENT　Sire, Mahon bon jour vous doint!
L'empereur vous envoie querre:
Si que venez a li bonne erre,
Puis qu'il vous mande.

CHATON　Et g'iray de voulenté grande,
Biaux seigneurs, a son mandement;
Je suis tout prest: ça, alons ment.　20

(Cato, with the two sergeants, goes to the palace)

Sire, en honneur noz diex vous tiengnent
Et vostre vie en bien maintiengnent
Par leur plaisir.

L'EMPEREUR　Soit ainsi con je le desir.
Maistre Chaton, vezci pour quoy
Mandé vous ay parler a moy:
C'est m'entente que je vous baille
Mon filz, pour apprendre sanz faille.
Dès ores mais, a dire voir,
Est assez grant pour concevoir　30
Ce de quoy l'endoctrinerés:
Pour ce dès ci l'en emmenrez,
Car je vueil que sache de lettre;
Si vous pri qu'en li vueillez mettre
Cure et entente.

CHATON　Chier sire, mais qu'il s'i consente
Et qu'il y vueille peine mettre,
Je le feray tantost clerc estre.
Or me dites, mon enfant douls,
A estre clerc metterez vous　40
Bien diligence?

(He turns to the Emperor's son)

LE FILZ [DE]　Oil, maistre, sanz negligence,
L'EMPEREUR　　A mon pouoir.

<table>
<tr><td>LE CHEVALIER</td><td>Il respont sagement, pour voir,
Com tel enfant.</td><td></td></tr>
<tr><td>CHATON</td><td>Par vostre licence et conmant
Me donnez congié, treschier sire;
Car je doubt que trop d'aler lire
Face demeure.</td><td></td></tr>
<tr><td>L'EMPEREUR</td><td>Alez, maistre, donc en bonne heure;
Or soiez de mon filz songneux.
Alez le convoier vous deux
Appertement.</td><td>50</td></tr>
<tr><td>DEUXIESME
SERGENT</td><td>Sire, nous ferons bonnement
Vostre plaisir.</td><td></td></tr>
</table>

(The sergeants escort Cato and the Emperor's son back to Cato's house)

*   *   *

(Cato's son is writhing in agony on his bed. Cato and his students gather round)

<table>
<tr><td>LE FILZ CHATON</td><td>Las! que je me dueil de jesir!
Las! de quelle heure fu je nez?
Las! trop longuement destinez
Suis a porter ceste langueur,
Ce meschief et ceste douleur
Qui si me menjue et desront!
Las! il m'est avis c'on me ront
Et c'om me destranche les nerfs.
Onques mais homme si divers
Mal ne porta conme je port.
En moy n'a joie ne deport.
A! pere, ne scé que je die:
Trop sueffre et port grief maladie
Par tout le corps.</td><td>60</td></tr>
<tr><td>CHATON</td><td>Biau filz, doulx et misericors
Te soient noz diex et propices,
Si que de cest grief mal garisses
Par leur bonté et leur puissance,
Et briefment, car au cuer grevance
Me fait plus que je ne puis dire;</td><td>70</td></tr>
</table>

Et ce que trouver ne puis mire
Qui y sache mettre conseil,
C'est ce dont je plus me merveil
Et de quoy suis plus esbahiz;
S'ai je fait querre en maint pais   80
    Conseil pour toy.

JOSIAS   Maistre, plaise vous oir moy,
Premier Escolier   Pour vostre filz, qui est mon maistre,
En qui nul ne scet conseil mettre,
Dont, par noz diex, c'est grant damage,
Vous vueil descouvrir mon courage.
En Nervie, dont je sui nez,
A un homme, ceci tenez
Pour verité et pour certain,
Qui est de si grant sainté plain   90
Et si juste sanz touz pechiez
Qu'il n'est grief mal dont entechiez
Soit homme ou femme, si le voit,
Que tout gari ne l'en renvoit;
Et ç'a il fait a trop de gent,
Sanz prendre salaire n'argent.
Si faites, sire, vostre filz
A lui mener, et je sui fis.
Quant le saint homme le verra,
Tout gari l'en renvoiera   100
    Et assez brief.

CHATON   Josias, son mal est si grief
Qu'il ne le pourroit endurer.
Penses tu qu'il doie durer
    Encore en vie?

JOSIAS   Maistre, de ce ne doubtez mie;
Je scé bien qu'il vit voirement,
Se puis deux jours tant seulement
    N'est trespassez.

DORECH   Maistre, riches estes assez;   110
Second Escolier   Je vous diray que je feroie:
Un joiau li envoieroie
Riche et bel en li suppliant

Qu'il daignast tant, vous suppliant,
Qu'il lui pleust a ci venir.
S'il tent au joyau retenir,
Il venra ci, je n'en doubt point,
Ou escripra de point en point
Conment pour santé recouvrer
Fauldra sur vostre filz ouvrer;   120
    N'en doubtez, maistre.

JOSEPHUS   Dorech a dit ce qui peut estre
Tiers Escolier Et doit par raison avenir:
Ou vous le verrez ci venir,
Ou le don ne recevra pas.
Envoiez y isnel le pas:
    Ce sera sens.

CHATON   Seigneurs, a vostre dit m'assens.
Querir me fault un homme sage
Qui sache faire ce message   130
    Et biau parler.

BUZI   Maistre, je m'i offre a aler
Quart Escolier Voulentiers et améement,
Se ne pouez miex vraiement;
    Je vous dy voir.

QUINT ESCOLIER   Maistre, je vous fas assavoir
Que, s'il vous plaist, de bon courage
Je feray pour vous ce voiage
    Tresvoulentiers.

CHATON   Vostre merci, mes escoliers,   140
Quant a ce pour moy vous offrez;
Ore un petit ci vous souffrez,
Et je revien a vous en l'eure,
Sanz goute faire de demeure.

(Cato goes to his treasure chest and returns with a money bag and a large jewel)

Mes bons amis, ça, vez me cy!
Tenez ce sac de florins cy
Et ce joiau, qu'est bel et gent,

Et si vous pri que diligent
Soiez vous deux d'aler le querre
Et de li doulcement requerre   150
Qu'il lui plaise a ce labourer
Que mon filz viengne ci curer;
Et que, s'il veult en ce pais
Venir, ne soit point esbahis:
Il ara robes et avoir
Assez; et pour li esmouvoir,
Tout ceci li presenterez
Si tost conme a lui parlerez
  Et de par moy.

BUZI Maistre, je vous jur par la loy   160
Que je tien, et par touz noz diex,
J'en feray mon pouoir au miex
  Que je pourray.

QUINT ESCOLIER Et je vraiement si feray;
Mais puis que ferons ce message,
Josias, or nous faites sage
Conment a ce preudomme nom
A qui portés si grant renom
  Et si grant los.

JOSIAS Valentin, seigneurs. Je vous os   170
Bien dire que, quant vous venrez
Au pais, plus y trouverrez
  Que je n'en di.

BUZI Alons men. Ains qu'il soit jeudi
Pense je si a exploictier
Que de lui saray, sanz doubter,
  Qu'il voulra faire.

QUINT ESCOLIER Buzi, chier compains debonnaire,
Ce chemin fas de bon voloir;
Mahon doint qu'il puisse valoir   180
A celui pour qui est empris!
C'est pitié quant il est espris
  De tel malage.

BUZI Voire, a ce qu'il est jonne et sage,

Et parfont clerc; ainsi l'entens.
Ore, ore! nous venrons par temps
En Nervie, si enquerrons
Ou Valentin trouver pourrons
          Que venons querre.

*   *   *

(The two students travel to the land of Nervie, seeking Valentine)

QUINT ESCOLIER   Nous sommes entré en la terre: 190
De savoir nous fault esprouver
Quelle part le pourrons trouver.
          C'est tout en somme.

BUZI   Paix! vezci venir un preudomme;
Ne scé s'il est de ceste terre –
Demander l'en vueil et enquerre.

(They stop a passer-by and make inquiries)

Sire, quel part demeure un homme
En ceste terre ci, c'on nomme
Valentin? en savez vous rien?
Dites le nous, si ferez bien,   200
          Se le savez

[LE NERVIEN]   Ne scé qu'a li a faire avez,
Biaux seigneurs; mais c'est un saint homme:
Ne se prise pas une pomme,
Ains est humble, doulz et piteux;
Maint cuer pervers et despiteux
Fait et a fait doulx devenir,
Ne peut malade a li venir
Qu'il ne garisse tout a net,
Quelque maladie qu'il ait,   210
Sanz herbes mettre ne racines.
Tant fait de belles medicines
Qu'il est le saint homme clamez,
Et de toutes gens est amez
Pour les biens qu'il enseigne et moustre.
Veez vous celle loge là oultre?

(He points to a humble dwelling)

Là de lui nouvelles orrez;
La nuit yla le trouverrez,
N'en doubtez pas.

QUINT ESCOLIER   Nous irons donc. Vezci le pas.   220
Biau sire, et la vostre merci:
De bonne heure vous avons ci
Trouvé si prest.

(The students go to Valentine's house)

BUZI   Alons men. Egar! avis m'est
Qu'a son huis le voi là estant,
Ou c'est un autre qui atant
A li parler.

QUINT ESCOLIER   Il nous fault esploitier d'aler
Jusques a tant que là soions.

(Valentine is standing at his door)

Sire, a vous droit nous avoions;   230
Enseigniez nous, s'il vous agrée,
Un homme de ceste contrée
Que par nom Valentin on nomme.
De la cité sommes de Romme,
Qui venons a li en message.
Faites nous ent, s'il vous plaist, sage
Par fine amour.

VALENTIN   Biaux seigneurs, Dieu vous croisse honnour!
Ne scé que li voulez requerre,
Mais tant vous di qu'en ceste terre   240
Ne sçay je omme nul qui le nom
De Valentin ait se moy non,
En bonne foy.

QUINT ESCOLIER   Sire, nous vous dirons pour quoy
Nous sommes a vous envoiez,
Puis qu'a vous sommes avoiez:
Le sage que Chaton on nomme,
La fleur de science de Romme,
De ce joiau que vous present
Et de cest or vous fait present,   250

Et vous supplie en amistié
Qu'aiez d'un fil qu'il a pitié,
Qui languist, dont c'est grans damages,
Car il est a merveilles sages:
Par maladie est touz contraiz,
Les nerfs a come touz retraiz;
Et il a de vous oy dire
Les grans cures qu'avez fait, sire,
Et que faites de jour en jour,
Si que plaise vous sanz sejour   260
Venir, li son enfant garir;
Et il vous voulra merir
Et guerredonner tellement
Que serés esbahiz conment,
    Tant vous donrra.

VALENTIN   Seigneurs, avis me convendra
Avoir dessus ceste besongne,
Avant que je plus vous respongne;
Mais je vous diray que ferez:
Par celle ville esbatre irez,   270
Puis que ci m'estes venu querre;
Si verrez l'estat de la terre.
De vostre present n'ay je cure —
Ce n'est a moy que paine dure
    Du regarder.

QUINT ESCOLIER   Mais il le vous plaira garder,
Sire, pour l'amour du preudome
Qui le vous envoie de Romme
    Pour vostre esbat.

VALENTIN   Or ne m'en faites plus desbat;   280
Certes, ja ne me demourra,
Li preudomme si le rara;
Mais vous irez, si com j'ay dit,
Esbatre en la ville un petit;
[Endemantiers] m'aviseray
S'avecques vous ou non iray.
    Seigneurs, alez.

BUZI   Bien, sire, puis que le voulez.
    Sa, alons ment.

(*The students wander in the nearby town as they are bidden. Valentine, on his knees, prays*)

VALENTIN   Pere des cieulx omnipotent,   290
Qui de nient le monde creas,
Et homme de fait recreas
Par la mort du benoit Jhesu,
J'ay par ta bonté, sire, eu
Grace de divers maux garir.
Et pour ce [m'envoie] querir
De Romme le sage Chaton;
Si depri, sire, ton saint nom
De tant de sens com puis avoir,
Que tu me faces assavoir   300
Si m'est bon d'aler y, vraiz Diex,
Et se le peuple en vaulra miex,
Et se point en croistra la foy
Crestienne. Sire, entens moi;
Tu voiz bien ma devocion,
Or respons a m'entencion:
    Que veulx que face?

*   *   *

(*In Heaven*)

DIEU   Sus, mere, sus! sanz plus d'espace,
A terre jus vous devalez
Et a Valentin en alez;   310
De par moy li dites en somme
Que sanz delay s'en voit a Romme.
Là par sa predicacion
A voie de salvacion
Plusieurs du pais attraira,
Et de servir les retraira
    Aux faulx ydoles.

NOSTRE DAME   Filz, j'ay bien toutes vos paroles
Retenues de point en point;
Bien li diray, n'en doubtez point.   320

(*Notre Dame turns to the two angels*)

Seigneurs, ci plus ne vous tenez;
Avecques moy vous en venez
    Chantant touz deux.

GABRIEL   Doulce mere au roy glorieux,
Vostre conmandement ferons,
Et devant vous chantant irons
    Joieusement.

MICHIEL   Disons ce ronde liement,
Gabriel, au partir de ci.

(Singing, the angels escort Notre Dame to Valentine)

Rondel

Dame, par qui grace et merci   330
Acquierent li cuer [repentant],
Qui vraiement sont lamentant

Des deffaultes qu'il ont fait ci,
Puis qu'a vous en sont dementant,
Dame, par qui grace et merci
Acquierent li cuer repentant,

Nous savons bien qu'il est ainsi,
Ne nulz n'en doit estre doubtant;
Car vous pouez troplus que tant,

Dame, par qui grace et merci   340
Acquierent li cuer repentant
Qui vraiement sont lamentant.

NOSTRE DAME   Valentin, sanz estre doubtant,
Va t'en a Romme la cité;
Car je te di pour verité
Que maint lairont la loy paienne
Et prendront la foy crestienne
Par ce que tu leur prescheras,
Et maint convertir en verras
A Dieu qui ci endroit m'envoie,   350
Si que sanz delay mett t'a voie;
Diex le te mande. Je m'en vois.
Chantez, seigneurs, a haulte voiz
    De ci partans.

GABRIEL Dame, nous ferons sanz contens
Ce qui vous plaira, sanz nul si.

(Singing, the angels escort Notre Dame back to Heaven)

Rondel

... Nous sçavons bien qu'il est ainsi,
Ne nulz n'en doit estre doubtant;
Car vous poez trop plus que tant,

Dame, par qui [*grace et merci*   360
Acquierent li cuer repentant
Qui vraiement sont repentant.]

* * *

(In the town)

QUINT ESCOLIER Je ne scé se pour mal content
Se tenra de nous Valentin.
Compains, je vous pri de cuer fin,
Alons savoir sa voulenté;
Je doubt que n'avons demouré
 Trop longuement.

BUZI Ralons vers li donques briefment,
 Sanz plus de plait.   370

(The students return to Valentine's house and wait at the door)

VALENTIN Pere des cieulx, puis qu'il vous plait
Que j'emprengne cestui voiage,
Je le feray de lié courage.
Et m'i repute estre tenuz.
Les messagiers a moy venuz
 [Je] vois attendre.

QUINT ESCOLIER Sire, plaise vous a nous rendre
Response lequel vous ferez:
Ou s'a Romme avec nous venrez,
Ou se sanz vous nous en irons,   380
Et a nostre ami porterons
 Chose qui vaille.

VALENTIN	Seigneurs, j'iray, conment qu'il aille; N'en doubtez point.	
BUZI	Or seroit donc de mouvoir point, S'il vous aggrée.	
VALENTIN	Oil, sanz plus de demourée Alons nous ent touz trois ensemble. C'est bien a faire, ce me semble Selon mon sens.	390
QUINT ESCOLIER	C'est le miex, et je m'i assens De ma partie.	
BUZI	Puis qu'ainsi la chose est bastie, Je vous diray que je feray: D'aler devant m'avenceray Pour savoir l'estat de noz gens, Et pour moustrer com diligens En ce fait sommes.	
VALENTIN	Je l'acors. Entre nous deux hommes Vous suiverons tout bellement Et irons a nostre aisement. Alez, amis.	400
BUZI	J'en voys, puis qu'a ce suis conmis; Et si vueil mon pas avancier.	

(Buzi travels back to Rome ahead of his companion, who accompanies Valentine)

*   *   *

(Cato's house)

	Pour vostre cuer, maistre, esleescier Vien je devant.	
CHATON	Bien puisses tu venir. Avant! Quelles nouvelles?	
BUZI	Quelles, maistre? bonnes et belles: Le preudomme Valentin vient,	410

A qui honneur faire convient.
Qu'il le vault bien.

CHATON Se Mahon t'aist, a combien
Peut il près estre?

BUZI A mains d'une liue, chier maistre;
N'en doubtez pas.

CHATON Encontre lui m'en vois le pas,
Je ne m'en vueil plus espargnier.
Seigneurs, venez me compaignier,
Je vous em pri. 420

JOSIAS Maistre, je feray sanz detri
Vostre requeste.

DORECH Je me tenroie bien pour beste,
Se n'i aloie.

JOSEPHUS Par Mahon, et je si feroie!
Avant, avant!

BUZI S'il vous plaist, j'irai tout devant,
Maistre; et si tost que le verray,
Sachiez je le vous mousterray
A veue d'oeil. 430

CHATON Bien diz. Va devant, je le vueil.
Et le me moustre.

(Cato and the four students come out to meet Valentine. Buzi points him out)

BUZI Voulentiers. Veez vous là oultre
Mon compaignon qui ça s'en vient?
Cel homme qu'il par la main tient,
C'est il, sanz doubte.

CHATON Ma pensée ennuit sara toute.

(Cato greets Valentine)

Chier sire, honneur et longue vie

Et bonne aussi sanz male envie
  Vous soit donnée.   440

VALENTIN Et a vous bonne destinée,
Sire; et, s'il vous plaist, m'enortez;
Qui estes vous, qui me portez
  Tel reverence?

CHATON Ja ne vous en feray scilence,
Puis que le m'avez demandé:
Chaton sui qui vous ay mandé:
Et puis qu'estes pour moy venuz,
A vous honnorer sui tenuz,
Et si est droiture et raison.   450
Alons men, alons en maison:
La bonne chiere vous feray,
Là ma voulenté vous diray
  Toute enterine.

VALENTIN Et g'iray de voulenté fine
Pour entendre vostre propos
Et pour prendre un po de repos,
  Car de loing vien.

(The party enters Cato's house)

✻ ✻ ✻

(Later, over refreshments)

CHATON Sire, puis que ceens vous tien
Et qu'estes hors de vostre terre. 460
Vezci que je vous vueil requerre:
Qu'il vous plaise prendre et avoir
La moitié de tout mon avoir,
Tant en argent come en joiaux,
En rentes, en draps, en chevaux;
Je les vous offre bonnement,
Et qu'il vous plaise seulement
Mon enfant guerir a delivre
Du mal qui tant douleur li livre
  Ja a long temps.   470

« 73 »

VALENTIN Chaton, s'il te plaist, or entens:
 Tes biens temporieux que tu m'offres,
 Qu'en tes huches as et en coffres,
 Ne quier je point, c'est chose voire.
 Pour ce qu'il sont bien transitoire,
 Qui ne durent terme n'espace
 Ne que la fleur du champ qui passe;
 Mais combien qu'aiez nom de sage,
 Je verray se de bon courage
 Veulz et de vraie entencion 480
 De ton filz la salvacion.
 Par mi ce que je te diray,
 Une chose te requerray,
 Qui est assez ligiere et breve,
 Et qui a faire point ne greve:
  C'est mon entente.

CHATON Sire, demandez sanz attente,
  Je vous en pri.

VALENTIN Je te requier que sanz detri
 Ton filz et toy premierement, 490
 Et toute ta gent ensement,
 Ou benoit fil de Dieu creez
 Lequel nous a faiz et creez,
 Qui appellez est Jhesu Crist;
 Celui de qui il est escript
 Qu'il nasqui d'une vierge pure,
 Homme et Dieu en nostre nature,
 Qui pour nostre redempcion
 En croiz souffri grief passion
 (Grief, di je, quar il y fu mors), 500
 Et qui souffri mettre son corps
 Ou sepulcre ou il habita
 Trois jours; puis se resuscita,
  N'en doubte nulz.

CHATON Sire, qui est cestui Jhesus
 De qui me preschiez telement?
 Je vous pri, moustrez moi conment
 Ce que dites soit chose voire,
 Et raison par quoy doie croire
  Qu'il soit ainsi. 510

VALENTIN La raison, Chaton, vez la ci,
Combien que tu savoir la doies
Conme clerc qui tant sage soies.
Ne liz tu en la prophecie
Qu'a touz a escript Ysaie:
Ecce virgo, et cetera?
"Vezci qu'une vierge sera
Qui enfantera sanz deffault,
Vierge, le filz Dieu le treshault,
Lequel Jhesus nommez sera; 520
Car il son peuple sauvera
 De leurs pechiez."

CHATON Sire, ce que vous me preschiez
Ay j'assez bien veu ou livre
D'Isaie tout a delivre;
Mais conment pourra c'estre voir
C'une vierge puist concepvoir
Et vierge pucelle enfanter?
C'est un point qui fait a doubter
 Trop malement. 530

VALENTIN Non fait, et te diray conment:
Tu doiz savoir qu'il est un Diex
En trois personnes ès haulx cielx,
Qui n'est qu'une divinité,
Une essence, une majesté;
Et toutesvoies trois personnes
Sont en ce Dieu, ainsi le sonnes,
Par qui tout le monde fu fait.
Or revenons a nostre fait.
Quant le premier homme pecha, 540
En tel deu nous trebucha
Que pur homme de le paier
Ne de Dieu le pere appaier
Ne fu souffisant, si avint
Que Dieu le filz homme devint;
Mais je dis qu'amours seulement
Fu de ce fait conmencement,
Et sains esperiz consumma
Qui du plus pur sang assomma
Une partie ou corps de celle 550
Vierge qui mere est et pucelle,

Ou fu de nostre humanité
Couverte la divinité.
Si que Dieu fu homs et homs Dieux,
Afin que tu entendes miex
Ce qu'en Ysaie as leu,
Lequel acquitta le deu
Et amenda tout le torfait
Que li premier homme ot forfait;
Et toutesvoies par ce filz   560
Fu fait, de ce doiz estre fiz,
Le monde et tout quanqu'il contient;
Et que noz corps venront a nient,
Et par ce filz resucitez
Seront, et puis touz excitez
De venir a son jugement,
Qu'a touz fera generalment
    Au derrain jour.

CHATON   Vous dites en vostre majour,
Afin que je l'entende miex,   570
Sire, que ce Jhesus est Diex,
    Si com me semble?

VALENTIN   Voir est: Diex est et homme ensemble;
Et si est espoux, filz et pere.
A qui? a sa fille et sa mere:
C'est a la vierge dont nasqui.
Conme filz, tant conme il vesqui
Cy aval, li obeissoit;
Conme pere, la norrissoit;
Conme espoux, de foy la vesti,   580
Quant elle a croire s'assenti
Ce qui ne pouoit par nature
Avenir: c'est que creature
Se daigna le createur faire;
Mais ce fist il pour nous attraire
    Plus a s'amour.

CHATON   Sire, plaise vous sanz demour
Qu'a vostre requeste et priere
Ce Jhesu Crist santé entiere
Par sa vertu doint a mon filz;   590

(He points to his son, ill in bed)

Et vraiement, soiez en fis,
Nous deus serons crestiennez
Si tost conme il sera sanez;
Et le croiray mon sauveur estre,
Lequel voult d'une mere naistre
Et souffrir en croiz passion
Pour la nostre redempcion,
Et qu'au tiers jour resuscita,
Et après ès sains cieulx monta,
Et qu'il jugera vis et mors: 600
A touz ces poins croire m'acors,
    S'il a santé.

VALENTIN   Ha! sire Dieu plain de bonté,
De cuer humblement te graci
Quant prendre te plaist ces gens ci
Au roiz de ta misericorde;
Car je voy que leur cuer s'accorde
A toy croire, amer et servir
Pour ta gloire en fin desservir,
Que leur vueilles, sire, ottroier.   610
Or tost, Chaton, sanz detrier
Alez vous là mettre a genoulz,
Et vous aussi, biaux seigneurs touz,
Et prier Jhesus qu'il nous face
Liez de cest enfant par sa grace;
Et j'avec li ci demourray,
Et aussi le deprieray
    Devotement.

(Valentine kneels by the boy's bed)

CHATON   Sire, vostre conmandement
    Vois acomplir.   620

(Cato kneels)

DORECH   Sy ferons nous de grant desir.
Seigneurs, a genoulz nous mettons
Cy et noz pensées jettons
A Jhesu filz du roy celestre,
Qu'il vueille le filz nostre maistre
    Santé donner.

(The students all kneel. All pray, imitating Valentine)

VALENTIN Doulx Jhesus, qui touz jours user
Seulz a nous en toute accion
D'amour et de dileccion,
Si com tu le paralitique   630
Par vertu poissant, autentique,
De ton seul vouloir garisis,
Et de flun de sanc retrainsis,
Ce dit saint Marc, aussi la veuve,
Par ta grace, ainz que de ci meuve,
Vueillez cest anfant ci garir
Et de touz poins son mal tarir
Dont il est si pris et attains.
Biau filz, tes mains un po m'atains:
    Tenir les vueil.   640

(The boy tries in vain to move his arms)

LE FILZ CHATON Certes, tant sui feible et me dueil
Que je ne puis, se ne m'aidiez.
Mourir voulroie, ne cuidiez
    Point du contraire.

VALENTIN Belement les vueil donc hors traire.

(Valentine takes the boy's hands in his)

Sa! Diex les saint et beneie,
Et la doulce vierge Marie
    Sa grace y mette.

(The boy sits up and then stands, completely cured)

LE FILZ CHATON Pere, vezci un homme honneste,
Juste, saint, du vrai Dieu sergent!   650
Venez veoir, ma bonne gent,
Conment le devons avoir chier:
Ne m'a fait, sanz plus, que touchier
De sa destre main, et vezci
Que sain sui, la seue mercy,
    Conme une pomme!

CHATON   Disciple du vray Dieu, saint homme,
Conment vous pourray je merir
Ce qu'il vous a pleu garir
Mon fil, que ci voi sain estant?   660
Je ne sçay; car s'avoie autant
Dis foiz com pourroie finer,
Que tout vous voulsisse donner,
N'aroie je pas satisfait
Assez a ce qu'avez ci fait;
     Ce n'est pas doubte.

VALENTIN   Chaton, s'il te plaist, or escoute:
Ce que j'ay a ton filz valu,
Ce n'est mie de ma vertu,
Ains est le da Jhesu poissance.   670
Aiez en lui ferme creance:
     Miex t'en sera.

CHATON   Je ne sçay q'un autre fera;
Mais tant conme je viveray,
Conme mon Dieu le serviray,
Et reni touz autres pour li;
Car je tieng et croi c'est celi
Qui a a humaine nature
Conjoint sa divinité pure,
Et souffert mort et passion   680
Pour l'umaine redempcion,
Qui nous venra en fin jugier
Et par feu touz les maux purgier
Et les quatre ellemens aussi;
Je le tien et le croy ainsi
     Et le croiray.

LE FILZ CHATON   De vostre oppinion seray
Et sui, pere, n'en doubtez, certes:
Moustré m'a par vertuz appertes
     Qu'il est vraiz Dieux.   690

JOSIAS   Nous touz aussi; et pour le mieux
Renonçons a la loy paienne
Pour tenir la foy crestienne
     Dès ores mais.

VALENTIN — Or vous fault donc pour touz jours mais
Avoir ou cuer un propos: quel?
Qui soit en perseverent tel —
Que pour dons, ne blandissemens,
Pour menaces, ne batemens,
Ne pour peine que l'en vous face,   700
Ceste foy de voz cuers n'efface,
Que Jhesus fil de Dieu le pere
Ne soit Diex, né de vierge mere,
Qui n'ot onques conmencement
Ne ja n'avra deffinement
     En deité.

JOSEPHUS — A croire ceste verité
Nous accordons nous touz ensemble;
Car soubz le ciel n'est, ce me semble,
     Chose plus voire.   710

VALENTIN — Or ait chascun en son memoire
Qu'il le serve et aint d'amour fine,
Si que sa gloire qui ne fine
     Puist desservir.

LE FILZ CHATON — Touz autres dieux pour lui servir
Reni; car je voy sanz doubtance
Que ce sont de nulle puissance
     Touz faulx ydoles.

CHATON — Seigneurs, aussi qu'en mes escoles
Je vous ay leu de logique,   720
D'elences, de dialetique,
Et d'autre mondaine science,
En quoy j'ay mis grant diligence,
Sachiez de touz poinz la lairay:
Dès ores mais ne vous liray
Ne ne vous apprendré clergie
Se ce n'est de theologie
Et de ceste nouvelle loy;
Car je scé clerement et voy
Que toute autre science est vaine;   730
Mais ceste a congnoissance maine
Du premerain conmencement,
C'est Dieu de lassus, et conment

Il est tout bon sanz qualité,
Il a grandeur sanz quantité,
Conment sanz estre mëu meut
Toutes choses ainsi qu'il veult
A son plaisir.

*　　*　　*

(*The Palace*)

L'EMPEREUR   Seigneurs, j'ay de veoir desir
Mon filz, et m'annuie forment   740
Que je ne le voi plus souvent.
Puis que Chaton l'en enmena,
Par devers moy ne retourna.
    Que veult ce dire?

LE CHEVALIER   Il n'en a pas le congié, sire,
    Par aventure.

L'EMPEREUR
(*He turns to the sergeants*)
    Alez, vous deux, bonne aleure;
De son maistre congié prenez,
Et ci present le m'amenez;
    Veoir le vueil.   750

DEUXIESME   Sire, nous ferons vostre vueil
SERGENT   Incontinent.

PREMIER SERGENT   Alons le querre appertement:
En delay plus ne le metton.

(*The two sergeants go to Cato's house*)

    Mahon vous gart, sire Chaton,
    Et voz genz touz.

CHATON   Or ça, seigneurs, bien veignez vous.
De nouvel me direz vous rien?
Conment le fait mon seigneur? Bien
    Fait, Dieu mercy?   760

« 81 »

DEUXIESME SERGENT	Oil; envoié nous a ci Dire vous que li envoiez Son filz et le nous otroiez, Si le demande.

CHATON

Mais seroit vilenie grande
A moy se je li refusoie
Ne se je contraire disoie.
Tantost ira. Josias, sus!
Et vous, Dorech et Josephus!
Pensez de vous tost avoier   770
A cest enfant ci convoier,
Qui de son pere est demandez,
Et a lui me reconmandez
    Treshumblement.

DORECH

Maistre, nous ferons bonnement
    Vostre vouloir.

PREMIER SERGENT

Alons ment sanz plus ci manoir;
    Trop demourons.

JOSEPHUS

Alons! Tantost a li serons –
N'y a que deux pas a aler.   780
Mais garder nous fault de parler
    Je devant li.

JOSIAS

Si ferons nous: n'i a celi,
    Au mien cuidier.

(The three students and two sergeants go with the Emperor's son to the palace)

DEUXIESME SERGENT

De tout ce dont avez mestier,
Sire, c'est de conseil loial,
Donner et de joie royal
Vous vueillent par leur courtoisie,
Et avec ce de longue vie,
    Noz diex pourveoir.   790

L'EMPEREUR

Filz, j'avoie de vous veoir
Grant desir: bien soiez venuz.
Conment vous estes vous tenuz
De moy veoir si longuement?

Je m'en merveil moult. Et conment
Le faites vous?

LE FILZ DE Bien, treschier sire et pere doulx;
L'EMPEREUR Vostre merci du demander.

(He beckons to the second sergeant)

Vien avant: je vueil amender
Le salut qu'a mon pere as fait;   800
Car il y a vice et meffait
En ce qu'as dit.

L'EMPEREUR Biau filz, en quoy a il mesdit?
Trop bien l'a fait, ce m'est avis.
Je vueil savoir par ton devis
Sa mesprison.

LE FILZ DE Sire, il a dit en sa raison
L'EMPEREUR "Noz diex"; et c'est une falourde,
Une mençonge et une bourde!
N'est qu'un Dieu, non!   810

L'EMPEREUR
(Sarcastically) Non dya! Et conment a il nom,
Biau filz, ce Dieu dont me parlez?
Dites le moy, se vous voulez,
Ysnel le pas.

LE FILZ DE Mon chier seigneur, n'avez vous pas
L'EMPEREUR Oy parler du saint juste homme
Qui en ceste cité de Rome
Est venu puis un po de temps,
Homme paisible et sanz contens,
Disciple du vray Dieu sanz fin,   820
Qui est appellez Valentin?
Conment le filz Chaton le sage
A gari de son griefe malage
En la puissance, en la vertu
De nostre sire Crist Jhesu,
Qui ès cieulx a pere sanz mere,
Et sanz pere ot en terre mere?
Par lui tenons nous ceste foy,

« 83 »

Ceste creance et ceste loy,
Qu'il n'est, a parler proprement,   830
Dieu que Jhesus tant seulement,
    Filz Dieu le pere.

LE CHEVALIER
(*Indignant*)   Ce n'est pas verité bien clere;
Car le pere au mains miex devroit
Estre Dieu que le filz, par droit,
S'il estoit ainsi qu'il eust
Cause en lui pour quoy il deust
    Dieu estre dit.

(*The Emperor's son turns to the three students*)

LE FILZ DE   Biaux seigneurs, a ce contredit
L'EMPEREUR   Respondez li tost sanz delay;   840
Vous estes clers, il n'est que lay
    En ce cas ci.

(*Josias steps forward*)

JOSIAS   Sire, vous avez dit ainsi
Que li peres devroit trop miex
Que le filz estre appellez Diex,
Supposé qu'il deust Diex estre.
Pour cest argu confondre et mettre,
Se je puis, de touz poins a nient
Je respons, sire, qu'il convient
Qu'il ait esté premierement   850
Un principe ou conmencement,
Par qui toutes choses creées
Sont et en leur estre ordenées;
Et aucuns sages anciens,
Arciens et logiciens,
Philosophes ça en avant
L'appellerent premier moment,
Acteur de toutes creatures;
Si font meismes voz escriptures,
    Ainsi le dient.   860

LE FILZ DE   Souffrez. C'est voirs, pas ne le nient;
L'EMPEREUR   Le philosophe ainsi le moustre;

Mais ycy vueil dire cause oultre
Pour quoy principe le nommerent,
Et premier moment l'appellerent:
Car le temps n'estoit pas venu
Qu'il se fust encore apparu
Ne conversé ça jus en terre;
Pour ce ne sceurent tant enquerre
Qu'il le congneussent a droit,   870
Conme nous faisons orendroit,
Qui l'appellons en deité
Une essance, une majesté.
En ceste unité que disons
Une trinité divisons:
Pere, sains esperiz et filz,
Et n'est q'un Dieu, soiez en fis,
Non, quant a la divine essence;
Mais ès personnes difference
Mettons nous, c'est chose certaine;   880
Car le filz, sanz plus, char humaine
Prist pour nous donner gloire ès cielx:
Pour quoy nous disons homme est Diex
  Et Diex est homme.

L'EMPEREUR
(*Growing angry*) Mon pouoir ne prise une pomme,
  Seigneurs, par les diex que je croy,
  Se ceulx qui tiennent ceste loy
  Et la sement par la cité
  Ne fais morir a grant vilté!

(*He points to the students*)

  Emprisonnez ces trois icy,   890
  Et après m'alez querre aussi
    Ce Valentin.

PREMIER SERGENT Sire, nous ferons de cuer fin
  Tout ce que nous conmanderez.
  Passez! Emprisonnez serez
    Touz trois ensemble!

DEUXIESME Livrer les nous fault, ce me semble,
SERGENT A Vuidebource le jolier;

Si en serons hors de dangier.
Menons les y.   900

(The sergeants push the three students into the palace prison)

*   *   *

(The Prison)

PREMIER SERGENT   C'est bien dit. Jolier, ça, vezci
Trois prisonniers que vous livrons!
Tenez, nous nous en delivrons;
Gardez les bien!

LE JOLIER   Avant! entrez ci! Se du mien
Menguent, ilz le paieront!
N'en doubtez, ne m'eschaperont
Mais de sepmaine!

DEUXIESME   Or nous fault aler mettre en paine,
SERGENT   Biaux compains, et si bien prouver
Que Valentin puissons trouver   910
Ou que ce soit.

(The two sergeants set out for Cato's house, seeking Valentine)

*   *   *

PREMIER SERGENT   Sueffre toi; s'il ne me deçoit,
Je le te mettray en tes mains:
C'est a quoi je pense le mains.
Alons men. Un po le cognois.

(They see Valentine in the street)

Egar! cel homme que tu voiz
Ça venir, le visage en terre —
C'est il! Ne le nous faut plus querre!
Alons le prendre.   920

(They go up to Valentine and seize him by the arms)

DEUXIESME   Sa, maistre! il vous fault sanz attendre
SERGENT   Devant l'emperiere venir.

Or tost! sanz nous plus ci tenir,
    Passez bonne erre.

VALENTIN   Dya! Je ne sui murdrier ne lierre,
    Seigneurs; menez me doulcement,
    Sanz moy tenir si lourdement,
        Je vous en pri!

PREMIER SERGENT   Or tost passez dont, sanz detri!

(They march Valentine swiftly to the palace)

*   *   *

(They come into the Emperor's presence)

Chier sire, Valentin avons   930
Tant quis que le vous amenons.
    Parlez a li.

L'EMPEREUR
(*Coldly*)   Conment, maistre? Estes vous celui
Qui le peuple avez enorté
De croire en un Dieu qu'a porté
Une vierge, si com vous dites?
Par mes diex! n'en serez pas quittes!
Ou ce qu'avez fait defferez,
Ou a mort vilaine serez
    Livrez briefment.   940

VALENTIN   Emperiere, premierement,
Tu qui loy dampnable soustiens,
S'a droit pensasses de qui tiens
La dignité ou tu es mis,
Tu te penasses d'estre amis
Plus diligenment que ne fais
A mon Dieu par qui tu fuz fais,
Qui est de toute creature
Createur et Dieu de nature,
    Ce n'est pas doubte.   950

LE CHEVALIER   A po que mes doiz ne deboute
Si que les deus iex te crevasse,

Par Mahommet, en ceste place.
Doit ainsi parler un tel homme
Com toy a l'empereur de Romme?
En male estraine!

(*The Emperor turns to the second sergeant*)

L'EMPEREUR Souffrez. Va tantost, si m'amaine
Ces trois compaignons qu'en prison
As hui mis pour leur mesprison
Cy devant moy.   960

DEUXIESME Sire, par la foy que vous doy,
SERGENT Voulentiers, sanz chiere rebource.

(*The second sergeant goes to the prison*)

* * *

Or ça! je revien, Vuidebource.
Ces trois prisonniers attaingniez;
Il faudra qu'avec moy veigniez
Pour les mener jusqu'a la court,
Et que nous les tenions de court
Et près de nous.

LE JOLIER Ne vous en doubtez, ami doulx.
Sa! entre vous trois issiez hors!   970
Ho! il les nous fault par les corps
Lier ensemble.

(*They tie the three students together*)

DEUXIESME C'est bien dit: aussi, ce me semble,
SERGENT Plus asseur les enmenrons
Quant ainsi liez les tenrons
Conme tu diz.

LE JOLIER Ainsi maine je court touz diz
Ceulx que je sçay qui ont meffait.
Avant! alons men. Tien, c'est fait:
Acouplez sont.   980

DEUXIESME   C'est voir: d'eschaper pouoir n'ont.

SERGENT   Avant, merdaille! Avant trotez,
    Se de ce baston ci frotez
        Ne voulez estre.

(The second sergeant brandishes a stick and, with the jailer, pushes the students into the Emperor's presence)

*   *   *

LE JOLIER   Vezci, mon chier seigneur et maistre,
    Les prisonniers que demandez.
    S'il vous plaist, or vous conmandez
        C'on en fera.

L'EMPEREUR   Assez tost on le te dira.

(He turns to Valentine in a fury)

    Truant, pour ce qu'as convertiz   990
    Ceulz ci et a toy pervertiz,
    Devant toy decolez seront!
    C'est le prouffit qu'il en aront.
    Avant! copez leur tost les testes,
    Puis lessiez aux sauvages bestes
        Les corps mengier!

VALENTIN
(To the students)

    Mes freres et mi ami chier,
    De la mort des corps ne vous chaille;
    Soiez fors en ceste bataille,
    Contre ce serpent combatez;   1000
    Car je vous di vous acquestez
    Gloire qui touz jours durera
    Et vie qui ja fin n'ara,
    Et par ce brief et court martire
    Verrez sanz fin Dieu nostre sire,
        Si conme il est.

JOSEPHUS   Homme de Dieu, nous sommes prest
    De faire quanque tu nous diz;
    Or prie Dieu qu'en paradiz
        Noz ames mette.   1010

VALENTIN Vostre voulenté sera faite
De bon cuer: j'en vueil Dieu prier
Ci endroit, sanz plus detrier,
 Mes chiers amis.

(Valentine kneels and prays as the executions take place)

(The jailer makes Josephus kneel before him)

LE JOLIER Tu seras premier a fin mis.
Passe avant, agenoille toy.

(He beheads the student with a sword)

C'est fait; il n'i a mais de quoy
 Jamais mot die.

VALENTIN Doulx Jhesus, en la conpagnie
De tes sains anges ces personnes 1020
Reçoy, et ta gloire leur donnes;
Si que ta mere et toy, filz, voient
Ainsi conme par foy le croient
 Ça jus en terre.

*   *   *

(In Heaven)

DIEU Mere, je vueil qu'aliez bonne erre
A mes amis que voi là estre,
Qu'on veult a mort pour mon nom mettre.
Anges, vous deux la conduisiez
 D'un biau chant faire. 1030

GABRIEL Vostre vouloir si nous doit plaire,
 Sire, par droit.

MICHIEL Nous en irons par là endroit
 Quand jus serons.

(The angels and Notre Dame leave Heaven)

*   *   *

(*In the Palace*)

(*The Jailer beheads Dorech*)

<table>
<tr><td>LE JOLIER</td><td>Sa, seigneurs, sa! de chapperons
N'arez ja mais, certes, mestier,
Mais qu'aie ouvré de mon mestier
Sur vous icy!</td><td></td></tr>
<tr><td>GABRIEL</td><td>Dites avec moy ce chant ci,
Michiel; ja repris n'en serez.</td><td>1040</td></tr>
</table>

(*The angels sing as they escort Notre Dame*)

Rondel

Venez vous en, benëurez,
Lassus ou royaume de Dieu;

En gloire sanz fin mis serez.
Venez vous en, benëurez,

Et touz jours sanz mort viverez:
Trop y a delictable lieu.

Venez vous en, benëurez,
Lassus ou royaume de Dieu.

(*The Jailer beheads Josephus*)

<table>
<tr><td>LE JOLIER</td><td>Or sçay je bien ne prescherez
Ja mais nul lieu nouvelle loy!
Chascuns est endormiz tout coy,
Ce m'est avis.</td><td>1050</td></tr>
<tr><td>NOSTRE DAME</td><td>Or tost, sanz plus faire devis,
Mes amis, ces ames prenez
Et ici plus ne vous tenez;
Mais conmans que chacun s'avoie
A nous en raler par la voie
Que venuz sommes.</td><td></td></tr>
</table>

(*The angels and Notre Dame take up the three students and escort them to Heaven*)

<table>
<tr><td>MICHIEL</td><td>Dame des cieulx, dame des hommes,</td></tr>
</table>

1060

> Fontaine de misericorde,
> A vo vouloir faire s'accorde
> Chascun de nous.

GABRIEL C'est voir. Pardisons, ami doulx,
Nostre chant tant qu'il soit finez.

(The angels sing as they go)

Rondel

... Et touz jours sanz mort viverez:
Trop y a delictable lieu.

Venez vous ent, benëurez,
Lassus ou royaume de Dieu.

*   *   *

(The Emperor is astonished by the celestial music all have heard)

L'EMPEREUR Seigneurs, escoutez! En quel lieu
Oy je de chant tel melodie?
Onques mais en jour de ma vie
Telle n'oy.

1070

LE CHEVALIER Le cuer m'a forment esjoy;
Mais dont ce vient moult me merveil.
Car gens ne puis veoir a l'ueil
Qui si doulcement chanter doient.
Il semble que près de nous soient,
A leur chanter.

VALENTIN Empereur, saches sanz doubter,
Ce chant que tu a tes oreilles
As oy, c'est – ne t'en merveilles –
La doulce mere au roy Jhesu
Et ces anges qui sont venu
Querre les ames de ces corps
Qui par toy gisent ileuc mors,
Qu'avec Jhesu Crist en emportent;
Et en les portant les deportent,
Conme oy as.

1080

L'EMPEREUR
(*Still furious*)   Conment? Ne te tairas tu pas
De ton Jhesu Crist devant moy?   1090
Vezci que j'ordene de toy:
Ou tu noz diex aoureras,
Ou par divers tourmens mourras,
   Je te promet.

VALENTIN   En Jhesu Crist du tout me met,
Si que ne me peuz tourmenter,
De ceci tu vueil j'enorter;
Car pour paine que me saroies
Faire, surmonter ne pourroies
La grant joie que j'en aray.   1100
Mais une chose te diray:
Se tes faulx ydoles et vains,
Qui touz sont de dyables plains,
Relenquisseiez et lessassez,
Et Dieu le vray seul aourassez,
Tu, qui est triste et en destrece,
Trouvasses joie sanz tristesce,
Repos sanz labour permanable,
Et regne sanz fin pardurable.
   Je te di voir.   1110

L'EMPEREUR   A ton dit peut on bien savoir
Que tu es plain de l'anemi.
Or tost, seigneurs! Tost, là en my
Celle place le despoulliez!
Quant tout nu sera, le vueilliez
Lier estant a celle estache;
Et puis le batez tant que tache
N'ait sur son corps blanche ne vert,
Mais que tout soit de sanc couvert
   Pour son chasti!   1120

PREMIER SERGENT   Si com de dit l'avez basti,
Mon chier seigneur, vous sera fait.
Sa, maistre! despoullier de fait
   Yci vous fault!

(*The sergeants strip Valentine and the jailer ties him to a stake in public view*)

Cy met on la table devant l'emperiere pour mengier

(A table is set before the Emperor and a meal served)

VALENTIN   Voulentiers, seigneurs; sanz deffault
Sui j'a vostre vueil? que vous semble?
Ne doubtez pas que de vous m'emble!
N'est pas m'entente.

LE JOLIER   Lier le vous vueil, sanz attente,   1130
En la maniere qu'ay apprise.
Est il lié de bonne guise?
Dites le moy!

(The second sergeant hands out sticks to beat Valentine)

DEUXIESME   Oil. Or ça! vezci de quoy
SERGENT   Il sera batuz, conme fol,
Dès les rains aval jusqu'au col.
Avant! chascun la seue prengne,
Et de bien ferir ne s'espargne
Sur ce dur dos!

(They begin to beat Valentine)

PREMIER SERGENT   Se sa char estoit toute d'os,
S'en feray je saillir le sanc!   1140
Je le vueil batre sur le flanc
Premierement.

DEUXIESME   Et je sur cestui, tellement
SERGENT   Qu'il y parra.

LE JOLIER   Je seray le tiers, qui ferra
Au long du corps!

(Valentine remains serene)

VALENTIN   Vueillez entendre a mes recors,
Entre vous qui me regardez:
Pour Dieu vous pri, ne vous tardez
De croire en celui qui me garde,   1150
Qui tout voit et partout regarde;

Qui le monde de nient crea,
Et par sa mort nous recrea;
Qui daigna d'une vierge naistre
Et a nostre semblant se mettre
Pour rachater l'umain lignage
Que Sathan tenoit en servage;
Qui de nous ot tant cure et soing
Combien qu'il n'ait de nous besoing,
Que pour nous en croiz mort pendi, 1160
Dont vie par ce nous rendi.
Congnoissiez le donc, congnoissiez!
Voz fauz ydoles delaissiez
Qui ne sont pas diex, mais sont dyables!
Ne les aiés pas agreables!
Servez le vray Dieu seulement
Pour qui je seuffre ce tourment,
Qui ne m'est pas torment, mais baing;
Car avis m'est que de doulz saing
M'oingnent ceulx qui ainsi m'atirent; 1170
Et vous cuidiez qu'il me martirent,
Et ce n'est que purgacion
Et ma glorificacion
  De corps et d'ame.

(As Valentine speaks, the fourth and fifth students come to the place and witness the scene)

BUZI Pere, benoite soit la dame
  Qui a nourreture t'a trait!
  Tu as tout ce peuple retrait
  D'enfer et l'as a Dieu acquis
  Par les paroles que tu dis,
   Qui voires sont. 1180

QUINT ESCOLIER Pere, escoute: ces gens ne font
  Mais que baptesme demander,
  Pour eulx envers Dieu amender
   De leurs meffaiz.

(The sound of a great crowd can be heard in the distance)

VALENTIN Soient en ce vouloir parfaiz,
  Il souffira a Dieu assez,

Tant q'un pou de temps soit passez,
C'on leur donrra.

PREMIER SERGENT   Par Mahon, mon seigneur sara
Maintenant ces nouvelles ci.   1190

(He runs to the Emperor, who is still dining)

Sire, je vous vieng dire ainsi:
De nostre loy sont perverti
Bien [set mille] qu'a converti
Valentin tant dis conme on l'a
Batu a celle estache là!
A brief, tout le peuple est creant
En son Dieu, je le vous creant
En bonne foy.

L'EMPEREUR   Va, fay l'amener devant moy
Yci en l'eure!   1200

PREMIER SERGENT   Sire, se Mahon me sequere,
Je vois.

(He returns to where Valentine is still being beaten at the stake)

Ho! seigneurs! sanz plus batre,
Mener le nous fault sanz debatre
A l'emperiere.

DEUXIESME   Si le menrons en la maniere
SERGENT   Qu'il est, mais que deslié soit:
Aussi plus est ci, plus deçoit
De gens sanz nombre.

(The jailer unties Valentine)

LE JOLIER   Voire, et si nous tolt et encombre
De faire ailleurs nostre prouffit,   1210
Et il mesmes se desconfit.
Deliez est, alons nous ent
Et l'en menons. Trop longuement
Sommes icy.

PREMIER SERGENT Alons!

(They bring Valentine before the Emperor, who is still dining)

> Mon cher seigneur, vezci
> Que demandez.

L'EMPEREUR
(Mad with rage) Ore, t'es tu point amendez?
> Di me voir de bon cuer ouvert!
> Au mains te voi je tout couvert
> De sanc. Que ne t'a regardé   1220
> Ton Dieu, et qu'il t'eust gardĕ
> De ce tourment, de ceste paine?
> Je te di – n'est pas chose vaine –
> Se je ne voy que tu laboures
> A ce que tu mes diex aoures,
> Je feray ci tes jours finer;
> Car le chief te feray couper,
> Je te di bien.

VALENTIN Tes jours sont plus briez que li mien!
> Je ne scé de quoy me menaces;   1230
> Je te di que tout au pis faces
> Que tu pourras.

L'EMPEREUR Par mes diex, en l'eure mourras!
> Vuidebource, sanz plus ci estre,
> Vaz le moy là hors a mort mettre;
> Et se tu voiz qu'il y surviengne
> Nul qui pour crestien se tiengne,
> Met tout a fin.

LE JOLIER Sire, par mon dieu Appolin,
> Voulentiers; n'en ara ja mains.   1240
> Sa, maistre, sa! puis qu'en mes mains
> Estes, gueres ne durerez!
> Passez! Assez tost finerez
> Honteusement!

(The jailer drives Valentine towards the prison. The fourth and fifth students follow)

<table>
<tr><td>BUZI</td><td>Pere, avant! viguereusement
Labourez a ce derrenier!
Conme bon, loyal chevalier,
Par la mort que tu souffreras
Couronne de vie acquerras
Sanz finement.</td><td>1250</td></tr>
</table>

QUINT ESCOLIER

Pere, qui cause et mouvement
Es que nous sommes crestiens
Et tenons la loy que tu tiens,
Moustre cy ta perfeccion.
Sachiez c'est nostre entencion
Qu'en quelque lieu que tu iras
Nous deux a compagnons aras
Et a amis.

(The Emperor suffocates at table; a bone is stuck in his throat. He dies in agony)

L'EMPEREUR

Un os s'est avalé et mis
En ma gorge, ci en cest angle!   1260
Seigneurs, certainement j'estrangle
Et suis a mort!

(Two devils rush from the mouth of Hell)

PREMIER DYABLE

Avant tost, nous deux par acort!
Sathan, prenons cest emperiere!
Il a tant fait ça en arriere
Qu'il est nostre par droit acquis.
J'ay assez de ses faiz enquis;
Il fault qu'en enfer le livrons,
Si que tost nous en delivrons!
Emportons l'en!   1270

DEUXIESME DYABLE

Il ne revendra de cest an
Ne ja mais, tant il a empris,
Puis que saisi l'avons et pris.
Et que l'emport!

(The devils gleefully drag the Emperor's body off to Hell)

<table>
<tr><td>LE FILZ DE
L'EMPEREUR</td><td>Seigneurs, plain sui de desconfort!
Car je voi yci que mon pere
A pris fin honteuse et amere;
Car en mengant s'est estranglez,
Et si sommes si avuglez
Que nul de nous, ce me recors,
Ne scet qu'est devenu son corps!
    C'est grant merveille!</td><td>1280</td></tr>
<tr><td>LE CHEVALIER</td><td>Mahon pitié avoir en vueille!
Car de lui sui moult esbahis.
Je croy que sommes envaiz
    D'enchanterie!</td><td></td></tr>
<tr><td>LE FILZ DE
L'EMPEREUR</td><td>Souffrez vous, a ce ne tient mie.
Ci endroit plus ne demourray;
Ailleurs querre manoir iray
Ou il ara plus seur estre.
Pensez de vous a voie mettre
Touz trois! Or tost, convoiez moy!
Au chastel c'on dit Bellevoy
    Vueil droit aler.</td><td>1290</td></tr>
<tr><td>DEUXIESME
SERGENT</td><td>Alons, sire, sanz plus parler,
    Puis qu'il vous haite.</td><td></td></tr>
</table>

(Exit the Emperor's son, escorted by the Chevalier and the two sergeants)

*   *   *

(In the prison, the jailer still menaces Valentine)

<table>
<tr><td>LE JOLIER</td><td>Valentin, il fault que la teste
Te cope sanz plus de respit,
Se ton Dieu du tout en despit
    N'as pour noz diex!</td><td>1300</td></tr>
<tr><td>VALENTIN</td><td>Je te di que j'aime trop miex
Que la me copes sanz demeure!
Mais donnes moy un petit d'eure
(Je ne te vueil plus demander),
Que je puisse reconmander
    M'ame a mon Dieu.</td><td></td></tr>
</table>

LE JOLIER
(*Reluctantly*)   Delivre t'en ci en ce lieu
                    Tost et ysnel.

(*Valentine goes on his knees to pray*)

* * *

(*In Heaven*)

DIEU   Sus, Michiel, et toy, Gabriel!
        Alez vous ent là jus en terre   1310
        L'ame de mon bon ami querre,
        C'on veult decoler pour m'amour.
        Je vueil qu'en gloire son demour
            Ait sanz fenir.

GABRIEL   Sire, sanz nous plus ci tenir,
            Nous y alons.

(*The angels go to Valentine*)

* * *

(*In the prison*)

LE JOLIER
(*Losing patience*)

            D'ainsi conme es a genoillons
            Ne quier que te lieves ja mais,
            Ne plus n'attenderay hui mais!
            Tu as assez ton Dieu prié,   1320
            Et si m'as assez detrié!
            Estens le col, besse la teste,
            Et pleures, se veulx, ou faiz feste!
            Tu ne m'en feras ja engaigne!

(*He strikes off Valentines head with his sword*)

            Tien! chevalier soies en gaigne;
            De moy as eu la colée!
            Je vueil en sauf mettre m'espée.

(*As the jailer tries to hide his sword, he is seized by the devils, who again rush out from Hell*)

Mahon, las! ou me suis je mis?
Entour moy ne voy qu'enemis
Hideux qui, sanz moy deporter, 1330
M'ont ja saisi pour emporter
 En grief tourment.

DEUXIESME DYABLE Nous te donrons assez briefment
Pour touz jours un nouvel hostel!
Sathan, compains, il n'y a el,
Ne m'en chaut s'il est clerc ou lay!
Emportons le tost sanz delay,
 Avec son maistre!

PREMIER DYABLE Ensemble les fera bon mettre;
Aussi sont il d'une convine! 1340
Avant! Avec moy t'achemine
 Ysnellement!

(*The devils drag the jailer off to Hell. The fourth and fifth students have witnessed the scene in amazement*)

QUINT ESCOLIER Buzi, or veons nous conment
Dieu veult ce saint homme vengier.
Je lo, sanz plus yci songier,
Que nous deux l'emportons bonne erre,
Et si le ferons mettre en terre
 Conme crestien.

BUZI Certainement, il me plaist bien.
Or sus! ne m'en chaut qui nous voie, 1350
Alons nous ent par ceste voie
 Droit en maison.

(*The two students carry Valentine's body to Cato's house, where it is received with reverence by Cato and his son; they put the body on the bed and as they do so, the angels raise it up and bear it to Heaven, singing as they go*)

MICHIEL Gabriel, sanz arrestoison,
Ceste saint ame ès cieulx portons.

« 101 »

Et en portant nous deportons
A chanter ce doulx chant cy:

Ordines angelici,
Cives apostolici
Et martires, lettate
Ab isto qui felici   1360
Sorte nomen amici
Dei cepit. Cantate!

*   *   *

EXPLICIT

SERVENTOYS COURONNÉ

On ne pourroit les grans biens declarer
Qui sont compris en la vierge Marie,
Car Diex la voult en sainte Anne creer,
Si qu'elle fut ains que née saintie
Au plaisir Dieu, qu'en li faire vouloit
Chambre de paiz et temple beneoit,
Palais d'amour, repos de sauvement;
Et avec ce y mist Diex plainement
Humilité, senz, maniere et raison,
Biauté, bonté, si que je di briefment
C'on ne pourroit trop essaucier son nom.

Que ce soit voir ligier est a prouver,   12
Car de Dieu fu fine purefiie
Pour ce qu'en li devoit encorporer
Fil, homme, et Dieu en une essance unie
Virginalment, dont bien appercevoit
Que Diex feist ce saint corps qu'il amoit
Digne, poissant, glorieux, noble et gent,
Et si sceut en son saint advenement,
Par signes vraiz plains d'inspiracion,
Si que li bon vivoient liement
En attendant de mercy le hault don.

Or di je donc c'on doit bien honnorer   23
Celle qui est de Dieu mere et amie,
Et c'on la doit de son droit appeller
Lune royal qui de biauté flambie,
Car aussi bien que la lune de droit
Prent ou soleil clarté qui l'en pourvoit,
Donna clarté la vierge dinement,
Li sains solaux du majeur firmament,
Car au saint ray d'anunciacion
S'ajoint a lui Diex qui est proprement
. . . .

Si que j'en doy bien ma dame loer,   34
Car c'est la lune en touz biens adrescie;
Et li solaux par qui elle luist cler,
Ce fu ses filz, le digne fruit de vie,
Li roy poissans qui Diex et hons estoit,
Vivant ça jus et ou throsne regnoit,
Et qui moru en croiz piteusement
Pour rendre vie et clarté a sa gent
Et enaprès sa resurreccion
En ame, en corps coronna noblement
Ma dame en qui j'ay mis m'entencion.

Dame gentilz ou il n'a qu'amender,   45
On vous doit bien nommer par seigneurie
Lune luisant, vraie estoille de mer,
Et le buisson de sainte prophecie,
Et la roÿne aussi qui ou ciel voit
La trinité, qui bien vous aime et croit,
Car là poez veoir en un moment
Un pere, un fil Dieu singulierement,
Qui de vous fist si noble assumpcion
Qui tuit li saint et saintes ensement
Sont resjois de vo doulce façon.

ENVOY

Princes, qui sert sa dame loyaument,   56
Amours l'en fait avoir bon guerredon.

SERVENTOYS ESTRIVÉ

Pour essaucier Amours et sa bonté
Fist Diex santir ains son advenement
La venue de sa nativité
Par la bouche Ysaie proprement;
Car il voult par prophecie averer
Qu'il naisteroit une vierge sanz per,
Qui fruit par ce fait divin conceveroit;
Et pour ce puis la vierge de son droit
A l'encencier comparer par raison
Et Dieu ses filz a l'encens de pardon
Qui les amans de plaisance pourvoit.

Dont doit avoir amant son cuer enté   12
A ceste vierge amer devotement;
Car c'est li encenciers d'umilité
Qui par un saint divin inspirement
Conçut, porta, enfanta sanz amer
Dieu tout puissant c'on peut encens nommer;
Et cil encens de paradis venoit,
Cil sains encens tout en gloire regnoit,
Cil encens cy par sa provision
Mist paix en terre et consolacion;
Ses noms loez et graciez en soit.

Si me merveil, quant g'y ay bien visé,   23
Pour quoy Juifs ne croient fermement
Que cilz royaulx encenciers sanz grieté
Conçut en li l'encens divinement.
Car aussi bien l'i pot faire esconcer
Dieu qui parti en deux la rouge mer,
Ou qui de rien creé le siecle avoit,
Ou qui la manne ès desers pourveoit
Aus enfans d'Israel par porcion,
Ou qui sauva Daniel du lion,
Au gré d'Amours qui faire le pouoit.

Si tieng l'amant de tresnoble eure né   34
Qui croit que cilz encenciers purement
Conçut l'encens de sainte deité
Qui puis fu mis en croiz amerement:
Là voult au feu de charité finer,
Là voult par mort les mors resusciter,
Là mist lueur ou obscurité estoit,
Là mist odeur ou orreur conversoit,
Là tint Amours en sa subjeccion
L'encens qui vint de la trine union,
Car bonne Amour a ce le contraingnoit.

Dame plaisant, souveraine en biauté,   45
Vraiz encenciers encensant doulcement,
Chascun doit bien loer vo dignité,
Car vous apportastes benignement
L'encens c'on peut en pain sacré gouster.
Cilz encens voult au peuple doctriner
La loy que Diex li peres envoioit,
Cilz encens ci plana en grief destroit
L'amer venin de no dampnacion,
Et nous donna pour mort purgacion,
Dont li miens cuers Amours loer en doit.

ENVOY

Princes du Pui, qui sert et aime et croit   56
Cel encencier par vraie affecion,
Par cel encens reçoit si noble don
Que cuer humains nombrer ne le pourroit.

NOTES

La Nonne qui laissa son abbaie

2 *grant feste*: 'a feast day', i.e. a day needing special celebration; this gives
   special motivation to the arrival of the preacher from a neighbouring
   monastery, and to his sermon, which is integrated into the action as the
   knight waits impatiently for it to end.
6 The nuns in particular are characterized by invocations of God, the Virgin
   and various Christian saints, just as in *Saint Valentin* the pagans are
   characterized by invocations of Mahomet.
18 *heures*: The Canonical Hours of the Office are: Matins, Lauds, Prime,
   Terce, Sext, None, Vespers, Compline.
30 *prime*: is sung at 6.0 a.m.
43–51 The precious vocabulary of courtly love used by the knight at this
   stage contrasts strongly with the liturgical atmosphere of the service in
   the chapel.
55 *prieuse*: the rhyme scheme forces this variant of *prieure* 'Prioress', i.e. the
   Superior of a Convent; the second nun is therefore relatively junior.

SERMON

[1] Luke I, 29 'And when she saw him, she was troubled at his saying, and
   cast in her mind what manner of salutation this should be.' This quota-
   tion refers to the Annunciation.
[3] *Doulce gent*: a conventional opening to the sermon, after the text, and one
   of several characteristic touches of style which suggest that the sermon
   was, indeed, composed and preached by a priest, as the plays themselves
   may well have been.
[9] The complete prayer *Ave Maria* should probably be recited here; see lines
   357–359.
[16] *elles craingnent a la foiz les choses seures*: the text and the commentary on it
   is relevant to the play in that the second nun, when she is twice pre-
   vented from leaving the convent by the Virgin, refuses to believe in this
   'chose seure' for her own selfish reasons, but eventually has to admit the
   truth and come back into the fold.
[27–28] Luke I, 28 'And the angel came in unto her, and said, Hail, thou that
   art highly favoured, the Lord is with thee: blessed art thou among
   women.'
[41–51] This is a rather loose paraphrase of the Annunciation passage in
   Luke I.

[52] *saint Bernart*: Saint Bernard, abbot of Clairvaux.

[56–57] Matthew I, 21 'for he shall save his people from their sins'.

[57] *pour quoy?*: The rhetorical question is another characteristic trait of sermon style.

66 Note the contrast between the knight's impatience at the length of the sermon and the nuns' appreciation of its spiritual content.

113 MS *Et sainte*

128 *le saint baron de Galice*: St. James of Compostella, one of the most revered saints of the Middle Ages.

168 The knight gives vent to his distress by taking it out on his unoffending squire, in a flash of bad temper.

206 MS *devez*

218 *jeu parti*: the 'debating' poem of the Trouvères, but here used in the sense of 'bargain'.

219 MS *Je sui*

250–253 The knight here sings a three-line popular refrain with seven syllables to the line; this is unidentified, but for performance might be fitted to the music of some early fourteenth-century Rondeau on the same pattern, for example the monodic *Belle et noble, a bonne estrainne* of Jehan de Lescurel (ed. N. Wilkins, *The Works of Jehan de Lescurel*, CMM 30, American Institute of Musicology, 1966, p. 9).

254 *Venir*: The knight picks up the last word of the song.

260 *la dame de Bouloigne*: Boulogne-sur-Mer was a popular place of pilgrimage to invoke the *Dame* or *Mère Dieu de Boulogne*; better known to Parisians, however, was the church of Notre-Dame-de-Boulogne built at Menus-Lès-Saint-Cloud by Philippe IV and later known to be the seat of a *confrérie*.

264 'And we have come to a firm agreement'.

276 A note of dramatic irony enters here and persists through the subsequent action.

294–295 These lines indicate that the action takes place in mid-summer.

326 *tout de nouvel*: The Rondeau could indeed be a new, specially composed (or adapted) piece for 1345; it is on the eight-line pattern and does not occur elsewhere.

327 MS *Sanz retraire*

362 The action here is best explained by having the Virgin substitute herself for the statue when she arrives in the chapel.

371 MS *En dortoir*

390 The reference to '*deux nuiz*' in line 487 shows that the action is resumed here after some indication that the first night and a second day have passed before the second attempt to leave the abbey.

390–391 *desvé / enfantosmée*: there is a point of contact with the sermon here, for the preacher had insisted on Mary's *doubting* the appearance of the angel, and the nun here doubts her vision of the Virgin.

420 *un tout nouvel*: This Rondeau, like the earlier one, may well be one genuinely composed for the play.

423 *sanz decort*: this could mean 'with no dissonance', implying a simple harmonized setting, or "with no wrong notes', in which case a monodic setting performed by the two angels in unison would be a possibility. In the latter case music by Jehan de Lescurel might well be used again – his Rondeau *Dame, par vo dous regart* has the same structure (ed. N. Wilkins, *op. cit.*, p. 15).

425 MS *Gabriel bel est a dire*

434–435 *j'ay oy la vois | De l'aloete*: This is a rare reference to nature, but may also be a deliberate linking device; the squire has heard the celestial music perhaps and *interpreted* it as the song of the lark. Cf. *Saint Valentin*, lines 1069–1072, where the Emperor is puzzled by the music he has heard.

449 *Noz heures*: Lines 467–472 show that the Office in question is Matins, which is to be sung in 'the second half of the night', i.e. in the early hours of the morning.

452 MS *a suer*

467–472 This antiphonal exchange is the opening of the Divine Office of Matins; for the Gregorian chant, consult the Breviary. The source is Psalm LI, 15.

743 *diner*: used here as a synonym of *dejeuner* 'to break one's fast'.

476 *Sus la vesprée*: 'At nightfall'; the day in the abbey, with all its various Offices, is abbreviated for dramatic purposes. Cf. Notes to line 543.

487 See Notes to line 390.

495 *conte de Foiz*: in 1345 (the date of our play) the Count of Foix (and Viscount of Béarn) was Gaston III, later to be renowned as a soldier, statesman and patron of the arts and known as Gaston Phoebus. In 1345, however, he was aged fifteen and had only succeeded his father, Gaston II, in 1343.

511 MS *Dame ce soit*

515–528 This speech marks the turning point of the nun's desertion of the Virgin and is calculated to stir up the disapproval of the audience.

528 *en autre harnoys*: i.e. married to the knight, not to Christ.

543 'It is time to go to bed', but, strictly, the nuns have only just breakfasted after Matins in the early hours of the morning. Cf. Notes to line 476.

548 *chappitre*: 'General assembly', in other words another special day, with special preparations to be made.

553 'What must be must be'.

554 This line is the traditional opening of a poem of complaint or lament: Cf. Le Châtelain de Coucy –

> A vous, amant, plus k'a nulle autre gent,
> Est bien raisons que ma doleur conplaigne . . .

or Chaucer –

> To you, purse, and to none other wight,
> Complain I, for ye be my lady dear!

561 *une essoine*: the 'obstacle' is deliberately left unspecified, so that the ex-

planation may be reserved, with full dramatic force, for the moment of the nun's repentance thirty years later, lines 924–946.

583 *kyrielle*: an extension in meaning, 'some prayer or other'.

588 This tense and dramatic moment is enhanced by the agitated repetition.

616 *chanter*: probably again in the early hours, for Matins.

641–646 We here see the overall Catholic view: to sin and repent is almost more worthy than not to sin at all. That Satan should seek out the most saintly persons to torture with his greatest temptations restores the nun to a position of sympathy in the eyes of the audience.

658 *si lonc temps*: at this point it may be deduced that the knight and the nun have been married for twenty years.

660 *qui ja sont grans*: The ages of the two sons are awkward to calculate: the marriage lasted thirty years and the children were already '*grans*' before the knight's ten-year absence at the wars. It is unwise to pay too much attention to such detail in mediaeval texts: if we work it out strictly we have to accept that the children were not born until very late in the marriage (after sixteen years or more!) and that in the final scene they are aged, say, thirteen and eleven.

677–684 The rôle of the damoiselle tends to be superfluous, though having a maidservant shows the nun's increased status. This speech, however, stresses the enormous worldly benefits the nun's marriage has brought her, and therefore eventually makes her repentance and sacrifice of these advantages seem all the more admirable.

686 *saint Martin*: Saint Martin, Bishop of Tours.

697 The rubric here calls the DEUXIESME NONNE 'LA DAME'; this inconsistency is also present in the original MS list of personages, where it gives the impression that these are separate characters (and that there are additional nuns apart from the three principal players). The rubrics in our text edition, including those of *Saint Valentin*, have been made consistent.

722 MS *menger*

728 The whole of this scene has obvious entertainment value: a lavish castle; banqueting; minstrels. Although no specific stage instruction is given, the invitation to a musical (and maybe acrobatic) interlude seems clear. Popular dance music could be used (see, for example, the record Archiv 14018: seventeen anonymous dances from the thirteenth and fourteenth centuries) or some gay songs (e.g. by Lescurel or Machaut) would be in keeping with the atmosphere.

740 The knight is vassal to his overlord, the Count, in the normal mediaeval chain of feudal loyalties. A vassal was bound to help his overlord in time of strife, in return for protection at other times.

747 *Mourée*: Morea, the name given to the Peloponnesos after the Latin Conquest (1205) and thereafter often applied to that part of Greece. In 1210 Geoffrey de Villehardouin obtained the title of 'Prince'; in the fourteenth century much of the region was reclaimed by the Byzantines and in 1349 Manuel Cantacuzenus was sent to govern it as a despot. The principality of Morea lasted until 1430. Clearly the power struggle between Christian and heathen forces was very much in the news at the

time our play was being written (1345). We have here, then, a touch of the religious conflict which so dominates *Saint Valentin*.

775–780 The knight shows his worth in his instant acceptance of his feudal obligations, severe though the cost may be. Any hesitation would be a serious flaw in character in mediaeval eyes; his wife can only support him in his decision.

794 MS *N'ot*

802 See Notes to line 660.

823 *Loncval*: a place name of no special significance, chosen for the rhyme; there are two places of this name in Normandy (Eure).

838 The turning point of the action is announced here.

848 *sanz discorde*: Cf. Notes to line 423.

857–858 Note the vigour of Notre Dame's appeal: *Or sus* is repeated four times in two lines in her passionate exhortation, taken up again in line 865, and strengthened by the imperative *Vien* in line 870.

871 A direct threat of punishment to come if the nun does not repent.

880 *pardire*: 'finish off', i.e. by singing the second half only.

882 *accorde*: Cf. Notes to line 423.

891 This line is a variant of the first line of the preceding Rondeau refrain (e.g. line 885); this is interesting in that it shows a deliberate effort to integrate the religious Rondeau, whether specially composed or not, into the main action.

899 *le doulx roy haultismes*: i.e. Christ.

908 Since the knight has just returned from a ten-year absence (line 794) it follows that the marriage had previously lasted twenty years.

918 Cf. lines 376, 488.

921 *folement*: Cf. line 865, the nun takes up the word *fole* used by the Virgin.

923 Cf. Notes to line 561.

943 *mondaine amour*: Divine love is seen as superior to human love; love for Christ cannot be shared with love for a human partner.

952 *nonne*: 'past None' (the Canonical hour sung at 3.0 p.m.), i.e. 'our youth is past'.

954–955 The anticipation of a life of penance and self-mortification shows that the nun's return to the abbey is no easy decision, which makes her sacrifice more admirable and glorious in the end.

967–968 To atone for having taken the nun from a cloistered life, the knight will himself enter the cloisters, i.e. as a monk; there is an obvious sense of justice in this.

983 *con nice*: the knight's self-description here marks his complete evolution from early impetuosity.

987 This scene is an excellent depiction of the anxiety of two children missing their parents: it is characterised especially by ejaculations, repeated questions and, we may imagine, by general weeping and wailing.

1029–1036: A realistic passage as the squire tries to stop the youngest son from crying.

1037 *seur*: the knight significantly now no longer calls the nun his wife or *dame*.

1042 MS *requier est*
1052 MS *qua*[*n*]*t*
1055 *des draps de ceens*: i.e. nun's robes.
1081–1082 God's mercy is infinite.
1085 Proverb: 'Good deeds will reap their own reward.'
1093 The knight's wealth and position has been deliberately emphasized
to make his final contrition, as well as that of the nun, more note-
worthy.
1107 *Veni, creator spiritus*: this is a famous Latin hymn, Hymn 8 (Chant for
Benediction) sung in Second Vespers on Whitsunday; for the Gregorian
Chant, see the *Liber Usualis*. The text was probably composed by
Rabanus Maurus, Bishop of Mainz (d. 856 A.D.) and contains six verses.
The first verse in full, with translation, is as follows:

> Veni, Creator Spiritus,
> Mentes tuorum visita,
> Imple superna gratia
> Quae tu creasti pectora.
>
> O Holy Ghost, Creator, come!
> Thy people's minds pervade,
> And fill with thy supernal grace
> The souls which thou hast made.

This is the only Latin hymn not rejected by the Church of England and
is retained in offices for the ordering of priests and consecration of
bishops. In mediaeval times the singing of *Veni, Creator* was often
marked with special dignity, the ringing of bells, the use of incense,
lights, the best vestments etc., all of which gives us a clue to the tone and
manner in which the play should end.

Saint Valentin

SERMON

Cf. Valentine's preaching, l. 489 *et seq.*
[1] Proverbs XVIII, 19 'A brother offended is harder to be won than a strong
city.' The sermon here is far more erudite than that in *La Nonne . . .*,
with very copious quotations and a generally more ponderous tone.
[17] Saint Ambrose, Bishop of Milan.
[26] MS *esperituel*
[27] Saint Augustine, Aurelius Augustinus (354–430), Bishop of Hippo.
[34] MS *co*[*m*]*e*
[38] Psalms XXIII, 1 'The Lord is my shepherd; I shall not want.'
[40] Acts IV, 32 'And the multitude of them that believed were of one heart
and of one soul.'

[47] Matthew XXIII, 9 'And call no man your father upon the earth: for one is your Father, which is in heaven.'

[50] Malachi II, 10 'Have we not all one father? hath not one God created us? why do we deal treacherously every man against his brother, by profaning the covenant of our fathers?'

[53] MS *cree*

[59] Job VII, 1 'Is there not an appointed time to man on earth? are not his days also like the days of an hireling?'

[62] Saint Paul

[63] Ephesians VI, 11 'Put on the whole armour of God, that ye may be able to stand against the works of the devil.'

[73] Luke II, 35 'Yea, a sword shall pierce through thine soul also, that the thoughts of many hearts may be revealed.'

[76] Psalm XLV, 11 'So shall the king greatly desire thy beauty: for he is thy Lord, and worship thou him.'

[77] The rhetorical question is again much in evidence.

[78] *bougueran*: a linen cloth made in Greece and in the East; its colour here heads a list of symbolic shades representing various virtues, a type of correspondence dear to the Middle Ages.

[84] MS *paience*

[87] The Latin ending to the sermon is conventional.

1 This is a rare example of a line split between two or more characters.

2 *Chaton*: Dionysius Cato, an unknown moralist of c. third century A.D., renowned in the Middle Ages for his wisdom.

14 Cf. *La Nonne* . . . , Note to line 6.

21 *noz diex*: the plurality of pagan gods is stressed throughout the play; cf. line 808.

56–69 A striking speech, stressing the agony of the sick boy by the use of interjection and repetition.

71–72 The audience knows that pagan gods will be of no avail and confidently awaits the appeal to the 'true' Christian God.

82 The rubrics in the MS have been standardized throughout. Cf. Note to *La Nonne* . . . , line 697.

87 *Nervie*: A province of Gallia Belgica, named after the warlike tribe of the Nervii, subdued by Caesar in 57 B.C. The area covered the basins of the rivers Escaut and Sambre (N. France and Belgium); the journey from Rome is, then, about 1200 kilometers as the crow flies.

104 *il*: i.e. the holy man.

108–109 Presumably Josias has had news from 'home' (Nervie) within the last two days.

110–121 The Pagans show a simple faith in the power of riches and bribes; this is deliberately stressed in order to bring out the purity of motive and ascetisicm of Valentine.

160 The *loy* of the pagans is generally contrasted with the *foy* of the Christians. Cf. lines 346–347.

170 *Valentin*: Saint Valentine, Bishop of Terni, martyred under the Emperor

Claudius c. 273 A.D. and commemorated on February 14. Cf. the *Legenda Aurea* of J. de Voragine, transl. J.-B. Roze, ed. H. Savon, Paris (Garnier-Flammarion), 1967, Vol. I, pp. 206–207. Note the build-up of suspense by the withholding until this point of the saint's name.

174 *jeudi*: This gives us little indication of how long the students expect to take on their great journey, since we do not know on what day Buzi is speaking, but clearly he intends to take less than one week!

186 *Ore, ore*: The characteristic repetition adds to the excitement and agitation. Cf. *La Nonne . . .* , Notes to lines 857–858.

202 Rubric MS *L'Innermien*: 'an inhabitant of Nervie'.

222 *De bonne heure*: 'It was a lucky chance'.

238 From his first words, Valentine speaks of his *one* God, opposed to the pagans' several gods.

248 A reputation established more by the Middle Ages than by Cato's actual achievements.

266–267 The *avis* Valentine seeks is from above, i.e. he intends to consult God in prayer.

276 Cf. Notes to lines 110–121.

285 MS *Endematiers*

302–304 The action is now anticipated: Valentine's going to Rome must result in the conversion to Christianity of the pagan population.

313–317 This speech anticipates the later action even more explicitly.

329 The speech ends with a full eight-syllable line instead of the usual half-line.

330 For performance of this Rondeau it might be possible to adapt the music of a Rondeau by Guillaume de Machaut (1300–77), say, on the same structure: e.g. *Comment puet on mieus ses maus dire*, ed. L. Schrade, *Polyphonic Music of the fourteenth Century*, Monaco, 1956, Vol. III, p. 154. Instruments would have to be used, maybe off-stage.

331 MS *cuer lamentant*

346–347 Cf. Notes to line 160.

357 The second half only of the Rondeau is now performed.

360 The opening only of the refrain repetition is indicated, as was the convention, and the rest indicated by *etc*. The G. Paris (SATF) edition omits the final refrain line in error.

376 MS *Que vois*

421–430 Note the generally fair distribution of something to say between all the characters involved, giving a swift movement to the action.

462–465 Cf. Notes to lines 110–121.

472–474 Valentine makes no effort to hid his contempt for 'temporal goods'.

475 *transitoire*: There is a strong point of contact here with the initial Sermon, which stressed the transitory nature of worldly possessions and the enduring value of spiritual belief.

489 Valentine loses no time in commencing the conversion.

492–504 This speech amounts to a modified form of the *Credo*.

516 Isaiah VII, 14 'Behold, a virgin shall conceive, and bear a son, and shall call his name Immanuel'. Cf. Matthew I, 23 'Behold, a virgin shall be

with child, and shall bring forth a son, and they shall call his name
Emmanuel, which being interpreted is, God with us. . . .'

535 Cf. Machaut, *Le Lai de la Fontaine*, stanza 3b:

> Car cil troy font toute une essence,
> Une vertus, une substance,
> Un pooir, une sapience . . .

569 *majour*: the major proposition of a syllogism; the rhetorical learning of
Cato the scholar emerges here.

575 The rhetorical question characteristic of Sermon style is also frequent in
Valentine's preaching.

582–583 *Ce qui ne pouoit par nature | Avenir*: i.e., the virgin birth.

587 Cato seems a little impatient with these very difficult new concepts and
demands a more dramatic proof of God's presence: the curing of his son.

594–602 Cato here also recites a modified version of the Credo, containing
more than he has yet been instructed in by Valentine!

602 *il*: i.e. Cato's son.

630 Mark II, 3 'And they came unto him, bringing one sick of the palsy.'

633–634 Mark V, 25 'And a certain woman, which had an issue of blood
twelve years . . .', 29 '. . . and straightway the fountain of her blood was
dried up'.

670 *de la Jhesu poissance*: 'by the power of Jesus'.

676 Cato's conversion is complete. Cf. lines 316–317.

692 *loy paienne*: The (former) pagans themselves use the term *paienne*!

697–706 Here Valentine prepares the first three students in particular for their
martyrdom to come (lines 990 *et seq.*)

718 Cf. line 317.

719–738 Cato is abandoning all his secular learning and pedantry to preach
the gospel.

728 Cato still uses the pagan *loy* to refer to his new faith. Cf. Notes to line 160,
and lines 346–347.

740 *Chaton*: cas régime form 'to Cato'.

757 Note that Cato does not have the same reaction to the invocation of a
pagan god as the Emperor's son, lines 799–800. To do so would
destroy the action.

760 *Dieu mercy*: However, Cato does unobtrusively invoke the Christian God
in opposition. The sergeants do not seem to notice, unless the opening
Oil of line 761 is said in a quizzical way.

781–782 It is not clear whether Josephus' warning that the students should
remain silent in the Emperor's presence is out of respect for authority or
through fear of persecution.

785–790 The sergeant's greeting is deliberately flowery in style, with particular emphasis on the plural *Noz diex* in order to provoke the reaction from
the newly-converted Emperor's son.

799 The audience is left in no doubt here that Cato's (and Valentine's) new
teaching has had its effect.

803 The Emperor is taken aback; for the moment he is polite, for he had

genuinely looked forward to seeing his son, but soon shows his true colours as a cruel and intolerant tyrant.

814 *Ysnel le pas*: This barked-out order 'and quickly too' contrasts with the *Biau filz* of line 812 and shows the speed at which the Emperor is losing his temper.

820 *du vray Dieu*: The Emperor's son, through naïvety or through strong conviction, makes no concessions in his exposition of the Christian faith.

843–860 Here we have a very scholastic 'debating' approach from Cato's student.

855 *Arciens*: for *artiens*, i.e. maîtres-ès-arts, learned persons.

861 *Souffrez*: 'Allow me to interrupt'.

874 The nature of the Trinity is stressed yet again; this is clearly a point of the utmost importance, though the repeated explanation of such a difficult concept is harmful to the dramatic action.

905–906 I.e. if they are to have food provided by the jailer, they must pay (in advance, no doubt!)

908 *Mais de sepmaine*: 'Not in a week of Sundays'.

913 *Sueffre toi*: 'Allow me'.

923 The sergeants speak brusquely and are in no mood for niceties.

935–936 Obviously full of scorn.

942 *loy dampnable*: 'unholy religion'.

943–950 Valentine suggests that the Emperor is only in the position he is in because it is the will of the (Christian) God.

951–956 A fine speech of outraged dignity.

977 The jailer is keen to show off his professional expertise. The tying and untying of prisoners and actions of the jailer and sergeants provide excellent contrast with the 'preaching' elements of these scenes.

997–1006 Cf. Valentine's earlier preparation of the students for this moment, lines 696–706.

1015 *et sep.*: The interlinking of the beheadings, Valentine's prayer and the procession from Heaven shows a remarkable command of stagecraft and is visually full of fascination.

1023 *par foy le croient*: i.e. as the students believe.

1035 *et seq.*: A grim humour accompanies the beheadings.

1041 This *Rondeau* is well integrated into the play and fits the particular context of martyred souls rising to Paradise. For music, use might be made of a Rondeau by Machaut on a similar structure, *Puis qu'en oubli sui de vous, dous amis* (ed. L. Schrade, *op. cit.*, Vol. III, p. 161).

1065 The second half only of the *Rondeau* is sung here.

1069 Cf. *La Nonne . . .*, Notes to lines 434–435.

1080–1083 These lines could be interpreted as indicating that Notre Dame, as well as the angels, sing in procession, in which case the musical setting would be one for three voices.

1085 *Qui par toy gisent iluec mors*: It is probably more satisfying (and convenient) if the three students are *physically* escorted to Heaven, symbolizing the ascent of their souls. Valentine could then be pointing at some place on stage out of sight of the Emperor.

1095 *et seq.*: This confrontation resembles fairly closely the passage on Saint Valentine in the *Legenda Aurea*.

1116 The subsequent action indicates that the stake should be placed away from the Emperor's dining table and in a position exposed to the view of the general Roman population, so that the Saint's words and example bring about their mass conversion.

1125 The only original French stage direction in our chosen plays precedes this line.

1129 *et seq.*: In this scene the author spares no pains in conveying the blackest possible picture of pagan cruelty.

1147 *et seq.*: This speech must be addressed to an unseen crowd (off stage) who gather to see Valentine's martyrdom.

1177–1180 Buzi confirms the instant effect Valentine's words and example have had on the watching crowd.

1189 After such a scene, the sergeant's invocation of Mahomet conveys an almost comic effect.

1193 MS *.vij.M.*

1207 *deçoit*: the pagan point of view; cf. *perverti* in line 1192.

1220–1222 Cf. Matthew XXVII, 43 'He trusted in God; let him deliver him now, if he will have him. . . .'

1229 Valentine has the gift of prophecy: the Emperor will indeed die before the Saint.

1239 *Appolin*: With Mahomet and Tervagant this god makes up a 'pagan Trinity'.

1275 *et seq.*: The Emperor's son is a little disappointing in that he flees the scene with the unsympathetic pagan court officials. Clearly, nothing must distract our attention from Valentine at the very close of the play, but we might hope for some more satisfactory resolution.

1323 'Weep or laugh, it's all the same to me.'

1326 *colée*: 'slap' used ironically here.

1328–1329 The jailer invokes *Mahomet*, but takes the Christian viewpoint in describing the devils as *enemis*.

1334 *un novel hostel*: i.e. Hell.

1335 *Sathan*: Prince of devils.

1350 *Or sus! ne m'en chaut qui nous voie*: The Christians no longer fear persecution; cf. lines 782–783.

1356 This line has only seven syllables, matching the hymn following.

1357–1362 This is an unidentified Latin hymn. It is not part of the liturgy and is not to be found in reference works on hymnology. Perhaps it was specially composed for the play, for its sentiments exactly fit the context. This would confirm the impression that the plays, as well as the sermons and possibly even the *serventois* were the work of churchmen. The closing atmosphere of rejoicing resembles that of *La Nonne . . .*, where *Veni, Creator Spiritus* was sung; the answer to the musical performance of *Ordines angelici* can only be to adapt some similar piece of Gregorian chant to this text (or even compose some 'Gregorian' to fit it!) and, again, exploit effects of bell chimes and general brilliance.

Serventoys couronné: i.e. 'crowned', the winning entry.

It is worth noting, though it is to some extent inevitable, that the *Serventois* stress the points which have been so much emphasized in the play of the same year. It is not clear whether the poetry competition took place on exactly the same occasion.

33 MS line missing.

47 *vraie estoille der mer*: Cf. Guillaume de Machaut, *Le Lai de la Fontaine*, Stanza 4b:

> Hé! royne souvereinne,
>   Qui seur toutes luis
> Plus cler que la tresmonteinne
>   Ès obscures nuis . . .

56–57 This is the traditional *envoy* to the *Prince du Puy*, or judge in the competition. Taken alone the lines are amorous, but *Amours* in this context means, of course, adoration of the Virgin.

Serventoys estrivé: 'recompensed', the runner up.

1 Cf. the opening of Froissart's *Ballade*:

> Pour exaucier la haulte et noble estrace,
>   Ès biens d'Amours . . .

4 Cf. the Sermon which opened *Saint Valentin*, so rich in Biblical quotations and references, or lines 515–522 in the play itself.

9 *encencier*: Contemporary poets exercise great ingenuity in inventing images to explain the Trinity; cf. Machaut, *Le Lai de la Fontaine*, where he speaks of water being poured into a jug and frozen in a new form while retaining its original properties.

24–33 I.e. it is inconsistent for Jews to deny the Virgin birth and coming of Christ if they accept so many other marvels contained in the Holy Scriptures.

56 The *envoy* again follows the traditional form, but makes the religious significance more explicit than in the previous poem.

GLOSSARY

The selective glossary contains words likely to cause some difficulty. Apart from irregular forms, the masculine singular of adjectives, the singular of substantives and the infinitive of verbs are normally given, with reference to Miracle I or Miracle II and the line number. The first appearance only is generally listed for each word and the meaning given is appropriate to the context.

aage, *s.m.* age I 952.

accorder (acorder), *v.t.* to make harmonious I 120; to agree II 398.

accort, *s.m.* agreement I 264, II 1263; harmony I 424.

acheminer, *v.refl.* to travel II 1341.

acoupler, *v.t.* to couple, tie together II 980.

acquestez, *2nd pers. pl. pres. ind.* of *v.t.* **aquerre** II 1001.

acroistre, *v.t.* to increase II Sermon 26.

acteur, *s.m.* creator, author II 858.

adrecier (adrescier), *v.t.* to address, grant I 861; to accompany, provide with II Serventoys couronné 35.

advenement, *s.m.* advent II Serventoys couronné 19.

afeccion, *s.f.* affection I 114.

affaire, *s.m.* way I 1014.

affaittier, *v.refl.* to get ready I 569.

agait, *s.m.* ambush II Sermon 64.

agenoillier, *v.refl.* to kneel II 1016.

agréer (aggréer), *v.i.* to please I 286.

aignel, *s.m.* Lamb II Sermon 86.

ainçois (que), *adv.* before I 385.

ainçoys, see **ainçois** (I 96).

aing, *1st pers. s. pres. ind.* of *v.t.* **amer** to love (I 555).

ains, *prep.* before II Serventoys estrivé 2.

ains (ainz), *1st pers. s. pr. inp.* of *v.t.* **amer** to love I 43; aint *3rd pers. s. pr. ind.* II 712.

aisement, *s.m.* convenience, 'own speed' II 401.

aist, *3rd pers. s. pr. subj.* of *v.t.* **aidier** to help I 161.

aler, *v.i.* to go (I 98).

aleure, *loc.* **bonne aleure** swiftly I 845.

alier, *v. refl.* to unite, join I 959.

aloete, *s.f.* lark I 435.

améement, *adv.* amicably II 133.

amender, *v.t.* to make up for I 498; correct II 799.

amenuiser, *v.t.* to decrease II Sermon 22.

amer, *v.t.* to love I 92.

amer, *s.m.* bitterness I 82; *adj.* bitter II 1277.

amerement, *adv.* cruelly II Serventoys estrivé 37.

amistié, *s.f.* friendship, love I 147.

anel, *s.m.* ring I 146.

anfant, *s.m.* child II 636.

angle, *s.m.* corner II 1260.

annemi (anemi), *s.m.* devil I Sermon 7.

annui, *s.m.* trouble, annoyance I 6.

ante, antin (antain), *s.f.* aunt I 37.

aourer, *v.t.* to adore, worship I 361.

aourner, *v.t.* to adorn II Sermon 86.

apaisier, *v.t.* to put at peace I 969.

appaier, *v.t.* to appease, satisfy II 543.

appert, *adj.* evident II 689.

appertement, *adv.* promptly II 53.

appeticer, *v.t.* to make smaller II Sermon 22.

aprester, *v.t.* to make ready I 688.

aquerre, *v.t.* to acquire I 956.

arcien, *s.m.* learned person, Master of Arts II 855.

argu, *s.m.* proposition II 847.

armeure, *s.f.* armour II Sermon 63.

arrestoison, *s.m.* halt, delay I 58.

arriere, *loc.* **ça en arriere** in his previous life II 1165.

assaillir, *v.t.* to attack I 748.

assavoir, *loc.* **c'est assavoir** that is to say II Sermon 13.

assentir, *v.refl.* to agree I 669.

asseur, *adv.* surely II 974.

assommer, *v.t.* to unite with II 549.

assumpcion, *s.f.* assumption II Serventoys couronné 53.

atandre, *v.t.* to wait for II 226.

atirer, *v.t.* to ill-treat II 1170.

attaindre (ataindre), *v.t.* to affect II 638; to stretch out II 639; to take hold of II 964.

attraire, *v.t.* to attract II 315.

autel, *adv.* just as, in the same way I 770.

autentique, *adj.* genuine II 631.

autressy, *adv.* also, likewise I 735.

aval, *adv.* onwards I 696.

avaler, *v.refl.* to be swallowed II 1259.

avecques, *prep.* with I Sermon 27.

avenant, *s.f.* gracious (lady) I 132.

avenir, *v.i.* to come about; *loc.* **aviengne qui aviengne** whatever will be will be I 16.

avient, *3rd pers. s. pr. ind.* of *v.i.* **avenir** I Sermon 20.

avoier, *v.i.* to travel II 230; *v.refl.* II 770.

avoir, *s.m.* possessions II 155.

avugler, *v.t.* to blind II 1279.

ayse, *adj.* content I 443.

bailler, *v.t.* to entrust, give over II 27.

baptesme, *s.m.* baptism II 1182.

bastir, *v.t.* to arrange II 393.

béer (baer), *v.i.* to desire greatly I 318.

beneïr, *v.t.* to bless II 646.

beneuré, *adj.* blessed II Sermon 27.

benignement, *adv.* with kindness II Serventoys estrivé 48.

benoit (benoist), *adj.* blessed I Sermon 19.

besongne, *s.f.* undertaking, work I 259.

besser, *v.t.* to lower II 1322.

beter, *v.t.* to subdue, mortify I 955.

biau, *adj.* fine, beautiful II 1.

blandissement, *s.m.* flattery II 698.

bougueran, *s.m.* rough material, symbolic colour of chastity II Sermon 78.

bourde, *s.f.* silly joke II 809.

bout, *loc.* **mettre sus le bout**, to finish completely I 533.

braire, *v.i.* to cry, shout I 1015.

brief, *adj.* short II 1004; *loc.* **a brief**, in short II 1196.

briefment (briement), *adv.* swiftly, in short I Sermon 8.

buisson, *s.m.* bush (burning) II Serventoys couronné 48.

ça see **sa** (I 351).

ceens (ceans) see **seans** (I 279).

celestre, *adj.* heavenly I 621.

celi, *dem.adj.* that I 781; *loc.* **n'i a celi**, 'that is to be avoided' II 783.

cens, *s.m.* rent I 825.

cerchier, *v.t.* to seek I 768.

certes, *adv.* indeed I 122.

cestui, *dem.pron.* this (person) II Sermon 74; *dem.adj.* II 372.

chaasté, *s.f.* chastity I Sermon 62.

chaloir, *v.i.* to matter I 203; II 998.

chapperon, *s.m.* hood I 601.

chappitre, *s.m.* chapter meeting I 548.

char, *s.f.* flesh, sins of the flesh II Sermon 61.

charnel, *adj.* carnal, physical I 217.

chastel, *s.m.* castle II 1293.

chasti, *s.m.* punishment II 1120.

chastier, *v.t.* to punish I 1080.

chaut, *adj.* hot I 204.

chaut, *3rd pers. s. pres. ind.* of *v.i.* **chaloir,** I 203.

cheoir, *v.i.* to fall (I 66).

chevaleresse, *s.f.* wife of a knight I 398.

chevalerie, *s.f.* a valiant action II Sermon 60.

chevauchier, *v.i.* to ride I 764.

chief, *s.f.* head II 1227.

chier, *adj.* dear I 84.

chiere, *s.f.* face, countenance I 180; cheer II 452; *loc.* **de haulte chiere** with joy I 807.

chiet, *3rd pers. s. pres. subj.* of *v.i.* **cheoir** to fall I 66.

chiez, *prep.* at the house of I 1022.

ci, *adv.* here I 99.

cieulz, *pl.* of *s.m.* **ciel,** sky I 427.

clamer, *v.t.* to invoke, call I 410.

clerc, *s.m.* student II 38; **clers** *pl.* II 841.

clerement, *adv.* clearly II 729.

clergie, *s.f.* knowledge II 726.

cloistre, *s.m.* cloister I 524.

cloistrier, *s.m.* monk I 968.

clore, *v.t.* to close I 867.

coffre, *s.m.* chest, trunk II 473.

coiement, *adv.* quietly I 237.

col, *s.m.* neck II 1322.

colée, *s.f.* blow, slap II 1326.

compains, *s.m.* II 178.

complaindre, *v.refl.* to lament I 554.

comprendre, *v.t.* to include II Serventoys couronné 2.

concevoir, *v.t.* to comprehend II 30.

confesser, *v.t.* to confess, receive confession I 12.

confrarie, *s.f.* confraternity II Sermon 15.

confrere, *s.m.* colleague II Sermon 14.

congié, *s.m.* leave II 47.

congnoissance, *s.f.* knowledge II 731.

congnoistre, *v.t.* to know I 1011.

conjoindre, *v.t.* to unite II 679.

conmant, *s.m.* order I 875.

consummer, *v.t.* to perfect, consummate II 548.

conte, *s.m.* Count I 740.

contemplatif, *adj.* contemplating I 112.

contenance, *s.f.* behaviour I 123.

contens, *s.m.* opposition II 355; strife II 819.

continence, *s.f.* chastity II Sermon 66.

contraindre, *v.t.* to oblige to II Sermon 18.

contraiz, *adj.* crippled II 255.

contredit, *s.m.* dissent I 466.

convenancier, *v.t.* to promise, agree I 343.

convenant, *s.m.* promise I 485.

convenir, *v.i.* to have to I 546.

convent, *s.m.* convent I 580.

conversacion, *s.f.* conversation, communion I 113.

converser, *v.i.* to stay, frequent II 868.

convine, *s.f.* group, 'birds of a feather' II 1340.

convoier, *v.t.* to escort II 52.

coper (couper), *v.t.* to cut II 994.

courage, *s.m.* feeling, thoughts II 86.

courroucier, *v.refl.* to grow angry I 504.

courrouz, *s.m.* anger I 439.

court, *s.f.* courtyard II 12.

court, *adv.* tightly, 'on a short rope' II 977; *loc.* **de court,** tightly II 967.

courtois, *adj.* courteous I 198.

courtoisie, *s.f.* courtesy II 788.

coust, *s.m.* cost I 863.

coy, *adj.* silent I 307.

creance, *s.f.* belief II 671.

creanter, *v.t.* to guarantee II 1197.

crestienner, *v.t.* to baptize as Christian II 592.

crever, *v.i.* to dawn I 389; *v.t.* to gouge out II 952.

croistre, *v.t.* to increase II 238.

cuer, *loc.* **de cuer fin,** gladly I 539.

cuidier, *v.t.* to think; *loc.* **a mon cuidier,** it seems to me I 277.

cuisse, *s.f.* leg (poultry) I 537.

cuit, 1*st pers. s. pres. ind.* of *v.t.* **cuidier** to think I 378.

cure, *s.f.* care I 151; cure II 258.

curer, *v.t.* to cure II 152.

daignier, *v.i.* to deign I 937.

damage, *s.m.* pity I 640.

dampnable, *adj.* unholy II 942.

debouter, *v.t.* thrust II 951.

deça, *adv.* here I 813.

decevoir, *v.t.* to deceive I 636.

decoler, *v.t.* to behead II 992.

decort, *s.m.* discord I 423.

decoste, *prep.* beside, at the side of I 25.

deduire, *v.t.* to entertain II 1029.

deffault, *s.m.* lack I 752; sin II 518.

deffaulte, *s.f.* lack II Sermon 39.

deffere (defaire), *v.t.* to undo, recant II 938.

deffinement, *s.m.* end II 705.

deité, *s.m.* deity II 872.

delaiement, *s.m.* delay I 777.

delaissier, *v.t.* to abandon I 1094.

delez, *prep.* beside I 831.

delit, *s.m.* delight, pleasure I 217.

delivre, *loc.* **tout a delivre** freely, I freely admit II 525.

delivrer, *v.refl.* to hurry I 724.

dementer, *v.refl.* to grieve I 164.

demeure, *s.f.* delay I 454.

demour, *s.m.* delay I 502.

demourée, *s.f.* delay I 721.

deport, *s.m.* pleasure I 835.

deporter, *v.t.* to entertain II 1087; *v.refl.* II 1355.

deprier, *v.t.* to implore II 298.

derrain, *adj.* last II 568.

derrenier, *loc.* **a ce derrenier** at this supreme moment II 1246.

desavenant, *s.m.* mistake, misdeed I 613.

desbat, *s.m.* argument II 280.

desconfire, *v.refl.* to humiliate oneself II 1211.

desconfort, *s.m.* distress II 1275.

descorder, *v.i.* to fall out with I 890.

descouvrir, *v.t.* to reveal II 86.

desjuner, *v.i.* to dine I 1034.

deslier, *v.t.* to untie II 1206.

desoresmais, *adv.* henceforward I 954.

despendre, *v.t.* to spend I 129.

despisier (despiter), *v.t.* to despise II Sermon 43.

despit, *s.m.* scorn II 1299.

despiteux, *adj.* proud, despicable II 206.

desplaire, *v.t.* to displease I 497.

despoullier, *v.t.* to strip II 1114.

desroi, *s.m.* disorder I 431.

desront, 3*rd pers. s. pres. ind.* of *v.t.* **desrompre** to destroy II 61.

desservir, *v.t.* to deserve II 609.

dessevrer, *v.t.* to cut off II Sermon 19.

destranchier, *v.t.* to slice up II 63.

destre, *adj.* right II 654.

destroit, *s.m.* moment of climax II Serventoys estrivé 52.

desvé, *adj.* mad I 390.

detri, *s.m.* delay II 421.

detrier, *v.t.* to delay I 462.

deu, *s.m.* woe II 541.

deu, *s.m.* debt II 557.

deu, 1*st pers. s. p. hist.* of *v.t.* **devoir** to have to I 915; **deust,** 3*rd pers. s. imp. subj.* II 837.

devaler, *v. refl.* to descend II 309.

deveer, *v.t.* to forbid I 411.

devis, *s.m.* speech, 'own words' II 805.

dialetique, *s.f.* logic II 721.

diffame, *s.m.* slander, infamy I 222; dishonour I 638.

diffamer, *v.t.* to defame I 216.

dileccion, *s.f.* pure love II Sermon 16.

diligenment, *adv.* diligently II 946.

dinement, *adv.* deservedly II Serventoys couronné 29.

discorde, *s.f.* discord I 848.

dit, *s.m.* word, saying I 110.

doctriner, *v.t.* to teach II Serventoys estrivé 50.

doint, *3rd pers. s. pres. subj.* of *v.t.* **doner** to give I 288.

doit, *s.m.* finger II 951.

donnit, *3rd pers. s. p.. hist* of *v.t.* **doner** to give I 1026.

donques, *adv.* then, therefore I Sermon 43.

dont, *adv.* from where I 168.

dortoir, *s.m.* dormitory I 292.

doubter, *v.t.* to fear I Sermon 15; *v. refl.* I 749.

doubteux, *adj.* god-fearing I Sermon 14.

droiture, *s.f.* right I 520.

dueil, *1st pers. s. pres. ind.* of *v.refl.* **douloir** to be fatigued I 816.

durer, *v.i.* to last, survive I 439.

dya, *int.* heavens! II 811.

effraez, *adj.* frightened I 887.

egar, *int.* see here! I 68.

egarder, *v.t.* to look at I 453.

el, *pron.* anything else II 1335.

elence, *s.m.* debate II 721.

em for **en** (preceding labial), *rel. pron.* I 907.

embatre, *v.t.* to push in, force one's way I 150.

embler, *v.refl.* to escape II 1127.

emperiere, *s.m.* emperor II 1204.

empetrer, *v.t.* to obtain by prayer I Sermon 8.

empirier, *v.i.* to grow worse I 428.

emporter, *v.t.* to carry off II 1274.

emprendre, *v.t.* to undertake I 91.

emprès, *prep.* near I 714.

enaprès, *prep.* after II Serventoys couronné 42.

encencier, *s.m.* censer, incense holder II Serventoys estrivé 9.

encenser, *v.t.* to perfume with incense II Serventoys estrivé 46.

enchanterie, *s.f.* magic II 1286.

encheoir, *v.i.* to fall into I 317.

encombrer, *v.t.* to prevent II 1209.

encombrier, *s.m.* impediment, difficulty I 684.

encontre, *prep.* towards II 417.

encorporer, *v.t.* to embody II Serventoys couronné 14.

endementiers (endemantiers), *adv.* and *conj.* meanwhile I 30.

endoctriner, *v.t.* to instruct, teach II 31.

endroit, *adv.* in that (this) place I 124.

endroiz, *loc.* **en touz endroiz** completely I 879.

enemi see **annemi** (II 1329).

enfanter, *v.t.* to give birth to I Sermon 50.

enfantosmé, *adj.* haunted I 391.

engaigne, *s.f.* anger II 1324.

enlacier, *v.refl.* to be trapped, ensnared I 839.

enmy, *prep.* in the middle of I 171.

ennuier, *v.t.* to annoy I 501.

ennuit, *adv.* tonight I 499.

ennuiz, *s.m.* annoyance I 919.

enorguellir, *v.refl.* to be proud II Sermon 42.

enorter, *v.t.* to exhort II Sermon 62; to inform II 442.

enquerir (enquerre), *v.t.* to inquire II 187.

ens, *adv.* within I 695.

ensement, *adv.* likewise II Serventoys couronné 54.

entalenté, *adj.* willing I 320.

entechier, *v.t.* to taint, infect II 92.

entencion, *s.f.* understanding II 306; thought, belief II Serventoys couronné 44.

entendre, *v.i.* to intend to I 77.

entendre, *v.t.* to understand II 185.

entente, *s.f.* thinking, understanding I 93; intention 970.

enter, *v.t.* to graft II Serventoys estrivé 12.

enterin, *adj.* entire II 454.

entour, *prep.* about I 500; *adv.* about I 680.

entreaidier, *v.refl.* to help each other II Sermon 54.

envaïr, *v.t.* to attack, invade I 314.

envie, s.*f.* desire I 138.

erre, *s.f.* path, route II 10; *loc.* **bonne erre,** swiftly I 64.

ès (en les), in the I 431.

esbahir, *v.t.* to astonish II 79.

esbat, *s.m.* pleasure II 279.

esbatre, *v.refl.* to enjoy oneself, take pleasure I 500; *v.i.* II 270.

eschiver, *v.t.* to avoid I Sermon 15.

esconcer, *v.t.* to hide II Serventoys estrivé 27.

esconvenir, *v.i.* to be necessary I 324.

escripre (escrire), *v.t.* to write II 118.

escripture, *s.f.* scripture, writing II 859.

escuier, *s.m.* squire I 821.

esgaré, *adj.* stupid I 720.

esjoir, *v.t.* to gladden I 199.

esleescier, *v.t.* to gladden II 405.

esmaier, *v.refl.* to be dismayed I 635; *v.t.* to dismay I 981.

esmay, *s.m.* dismay I 489.

esmouvoir, *v.t.* persuade, move II 156.

espace, *s.m.* time I 118; pause I 651.

espargnier, *v.refl.* to spare oneself II 418.

esperdu, *adj.* lost, bewildered I 1118.

esperit, *s.m.* Spirit II 548.

esperitable, *adj.* spiritual, heavenly I 106.

espirer, *v.refl.* to be exhaled I 430.

espirituel, *adj.* spiritual II Sermon 16.

esploit, *s.m.* deed, exploit I 827.

esploitier, *v.i.* to act II 228.

esplouré, *adj.* weeping I 1071.

espoir, 1*st pers. s. pres. ind.* of *v.t.* esperer to hope I 1033.

esprendre, *v.t.* to take up, occupy I 92.

esprouver, *v.t.* t try to find out II 191.

essaucier, *v.t.* to exalt II Serventoys couronné 11.

essay, *loc.* se **mettre en essay** to attempt I 581.

essence (essance), *s.f.* essence II 535.

essoine, *s.f.* difficulty, obstacle I 561.

estable, *s.f.* stable I 822.

estache, *s.f.* stake II 1116.

estat, *s.m.* state, condition II 272.

estendre, *v.t.* to lay out, spread I 935; stretch out II 1322.

ester, *v.i.* to stand, be I 163.

estouvoir, *loc.* **par estouvoir** indeed I 917.

estovoir, *v.i.* to have to I 553.

estraine, *loc.* **en male estraine,** woe be to you! II 956.

estraire, *v.i.* to descend from I 221.

estrange, *s.m.* stranger II Sermon 56.

estre, *s.m.* state, condition II 1290.

estudier, *v.t.* to study, teach I 13.

estuet, 3*rd pers. s. pres. ind.* of estovoir (I 553).

esveillié, *adj.* bright, in good heart I 256.

eur, *s.m.* luck I 511.

eure, *loc.* **en l'eure** at once II 143.

euvre, *s.f.* works, deeds I 1084.

exciter, *v.t.* to incite II 565.

exploictier see esploitier (II 175).

façon, *s.f.* manner II Serventoys couronné 55.

faille, *s.f.* fail II 28.

faillir, *v.i.* to fail, lack I 9.

fait, *s.m.* deed I 110.

falace, *s.f.* trick I Sermon 24.

falourde, *s.f.* nonsense II 808.

fame, *s.f.* woman I 178.

fas, *1st pers. s. pres. ind.* of *v.t.* faire to make I 903.

faulra, *3rd pers. s. fut.* of falloir to be necessary I 1023.

fault, *3rd pers. s. pres. ind.* of faillir (I 414).

feible, *adj.* feeble I Sermon 17.

ferir, *v.t.* to strike II 1137.

feste, *loc.* faire feste, to rejoice II 1323.

festu, *s.m.* straw I 161.

fetis, *adj.* graceful I 127.

fiancer, *v.t.* to promise, assure I 344.

fichier, *v.refl.* to take oneself off to I 292.

fin, *adj.* pure, courtly I 147.

finement, *s.m.* end II 1250.

finer, *v.t.* to finish I 691; to pay II 662.

fis, *adj.* confident, certain II 98.

flambier, *v.i.* to burn, flame II Serventoys couronné 26.

flanc, *s.m.* side II 1141.

florin, *s.m.* florin, coin II 146.

foison, *s.f.* plenty I 542.

folement, *adv.* foolishly I 921.

folz, *adj.* mad I 318.

fondre, *v.t.* to melt I 519; I 1072.

forfaire, *v.i.* to trespass, transgress I 1074; *v.t.* commit sinfully II 559.

forment, *adv.* greatly I 369.

fors (que), *prep.* except for I 139.

fort, *loc.* a fort, grievous I 551.

fortraire, *v.t.* to carry off I 1044.

frere, *s.m.* brother, monk I 4.

fresle, *adj.* frail I Sermon 17.

froit, *adj.* cold I 204.

fuer, *loc.* a nul fuer, at any price I 44.

gaigne, *loc.* en gaigne, indeed, deservedly II 1325.

gaittier (gueter), *v.t.* to watch out for I 568.

garder, *v.t.* to look I 629; preserve I 697.

garir, *v.t.* to heal II 94.

generalment, *adv.* without exception II 567.

genoillon, *s.m.* knee II 1317; *loc.* se mettre a genoillons, to kneel I 460.

gent, *adj.* pleasant II Serventoys couronné 18.

germain, *s.m.* blood relation II Sermon 12.

gëu, *p.part.* of gesir, *v.i.* to lie I 869.

giste, *s.m.* lodging I 823.

glaive, *s.m.* sword II Sermon 73.

goute, *s.f.* drop, slightest bit II 144.

gouverner, *v.t.* to look after I 1012.

gracier, *v.t.* to thank II Serventoys estrivé 22.

gré, *s.m.* pleasure I 876.

grengneur, *adj.* greatest I 679.

grevance, *s.f.* distress II 74.

grever, *v.t.* to injure, harm I 811.

grief, *adj.* grievous I 945.

griefment, *adv.* grievously I 982.

grieté, *s.m.* pain, distress II Serventoys estrivé 25.

guerredon *s.m.* reward II Serventoys couronné 57.

guerredonner, *v.t.* to reward II 263.

guise, *s.f.* manner, way I 195.

habondance, *s.f.* abundance II Sermon 27.

haitiez, *v.t.* to please II 1296.

haitiex (haittié), *adj.* in good health I 784; I 801.

harnoys, *s.m.* harness, condition I 528.

haro, *int.* heavens! I 178.

haster, *v.i.* to hasten I 603.

hault, *adj.* late I 449.

haultain, *adj.* elevated I 1051.

haultismes, *adj.* on high I 899.

hen, *loc.* cheoir en hen (ahan), 'fall in pain', be struck down I 66.

het, *3rd pers. s. pres. ind.* of *v.t.* **haïr** to hate I 900.
heure, *s.f.* fortune, luck II 222.
heures, *s.f.pl.* canonical Hours I 18.
hoir, *s.m.* heir II Sermon 28.
hons (homs), *s.m.* man I 636.
hontage, *s.m.* shame I 517.
hostel (*pl.* **hostieulx**), *s.m.* house, dwelling I 664.
huche, *s.f.* box II 473.
huchier, *v.t.* to call to I 282.
hui, *adv*, today I 2.
huimais, *adv.* this day I 368.
huis, *s.m.* door I 296.

illecques, *adv.* there I 653; **ileuc** II 1085.
image, *s.f.* statue I 101.
incontinent, *adv.* at once II 752.
inspirement, *s.m.* inspiration II Serventoys estrivé 15.
ire, *s.f.* displeasure I 881.
isnel see **ysnel** (II 126).
issir see **yssir** (II 970).
issue, *s.f.* exit I 411.
istre, *v.i.* to act against, go out I 549.

ja, *adv.* indeed, now, already I 65.
jesir (gesir), *v.i.* to lie down II 56.
jeugleur, *s.m.* minstrel I 727.
jeu parti, *s.m.* bargain, arrangement I 218.
joiau (joyau), *s.m.* jewel II 112.
jonne, *adj.* young II 184.
jurer, *v.t.* to swear I 442.
jus, *adv.* on earth, down I 351.
jusques, *loc.* **jusques a tant que**, until II 229.

kyrielle, *s.f.* prayer I 583.

labourer, *v.i.* to work, endeavour II 151.
lace (lasse), *adj.* weak I 839.
laiens (leens), *adv.* there, in that place I 41.

lairay, *1st pers. s. fut.* of **laisser**, *v.t.* to leave I 968.
laisser, *v.t.* to allow I 90.
lamenter, *v.i.* to lament I 896.
languir, *v.i.* to languish II 253.
largesce, *s.f.* bounty, plenty I 253.
lasse, *int.* alas! I 635.
lasser, *v.refl.* to grow weary I 396.
lassus, *adv.* up above II Sermon 32.
lay, *s.m.* uneducated person II 841.
leesce, *s.f.* happiness I 597.
lerme, *s.f.* tear I 1072.
lettre, *loc.* **savoir de lettre** to be educated II 33.
leu, *p.part.* of *v.t.* **lire** to read II 556.
leyens see **laiens** (I 731).
lez, *prep.* at the side of I 311.
li, *pron. 3rd pers. m.s. cas régime* him I 90.
licence, *s.f.* permission II 46.
lié, *adj.* happy I 255.
liement, *adv.* gladly II 327.
lierre, *s.m.* robber II 925.
ligier, *adj.* easy II 484.
lignage, *s.m.* race I Sermon 25; lineage II Sermon 43.
liue (lieue), *s.f.* league I 69.
livrer, *v.t.* to deliver II 940.
loer, *v.t.* to advise I 29; to praise 1101.
loge, *s.f.* dwelling, hermit's cel 216.
los, *s.m.* praise II 169.
lourdement, *adv.* roughly II 927.
loy, *s.f.* religious faith II 160.
luire, *v.i.* to shine II Serventoys couronné 36.

machiner, *v.t.* to ponder, contrive explanations I Sermon 21.
main, *s.m.* morning I 763.
mainburnie, *s.f.* guardianship II Sermon 34.
mainer, *v.t.* to lead I 638.
mains (moins), *adv.* less I 428.
maint, *adj.* many a I 202
maintien, *s.m.* state, behaviour I 215.

mais, *adv.* ever, more I 910.

maishui, *adv.* this day I 360.

majour, *s.m.* main point II 569.

malage, *s.m.* illness II 183.

malayse, *s.m.* discomfort I 490.

malement, *adv.* seriously II 530.

mandement, *s.m.* command I 776.

mander, *v.t.* to command II 26.

maniere, *s.f.* bearing II Serventoys couronné 9.

manne, *s.f.* manna II Serventoys estrivé 30.

manoir, *v.i.* to stay, remain II 777; *s.m.* dwelling II 1289.

mantellet, *s.m.* little coat I 602.

marri, *adj.* sad I 585.

mater, *v.t.* to subdue I 955.

matin, *adv.* early I 547.

meffaire, *v.i.* to misbehave, I 671.

meffait, *s.m.* misdeed I 889.

meismes, *adj.* self I 898.

mençonge, *s.f.* lie II 809.

mendre, *adj.* lesser II Sermon 23.

menjue, *3rd pers. s. pres. ind. of v.t.* **menjier (mengier)** to devour, eat up II 61.

ment (men) as in **alons ment,** *defective locution* for **allons nous en,** let us be off I 34.

merci, *loc.* **la vostre merci,** thank you II 221.

merdaille, *s.f.* scum II 982.

merir, *v.t.* to recompense II 262.

meschief, *s.m.* distress I 911.

mesdire, *v.i.* to speak wrongly II 803.

mesmes see **meismes** (II 1211).

mesprendre, *v.i.* to behave badly, offend I 145.

mesprison, *s.f.* misdeed, error II 806.

message, *s.m.* messenger II 235.

mestier, *s.m.* duty, task I 302; trade II 1037; *loc.* **faire mestier,** to give a performance II 732.

meuve, *1st pers. s. pres. subj. of v.i.* **mouvoir** to move II 635; *v.t.*

mëu p. *part.* II 736; **meut** *3rd pers. s. pres. ind.* II 736.

mi, *poss.adj. m.pl.* my I 115.

mie, *neg. loc.* **ne mie,** not at all I 212.

mien, *poss.adj.* my II Serventoys estrivé 55.

mienuit, *s.f.* midnight I 380.

mire, *s.m.* doctor II 76.

misericorde, *s.f.* mercy, grace I Sermon 70.

misericors, *adj.* merciful I 1081.

moie, *poss.adj.* my I 837.

moine, *s.m.* monk I 1059.

mon, *term of affirmation used with various verbs,* indeed, of course I 294.

mondain, *adj.* earthly I 943.

monde, *s.m.* the world, wordly things II Sermon 61.

morir, *v.i.* to die II Serventoys couronné 40.

mors, *s.m.pl.* the dead II 600.

mortel, *adj.* deadly I 901; mortal II Sermon 59.

mot, *loc.* **a brief mot,** to be brief I 611.

moult, *adv.* much, greatly I 74.

moustrer, *v.t.* to show II 215.

murdrier, *s.m.* murderer II 925.

muse, *loc.* **paier la muse** to wait I 376.

muser, *v.i.* to loiter, hang around I 169.

my see **mi** (I 836).

naistre, *v.i.* to be born I 89.

nanil, *adv.* not at all I 12.

nasqui, *3rd pers. s. p. hist. of v.i.* **naistre** to be born II 496.

nepveu, *s.m.* nephew I 1047.

net, *adj.* pure I Sermon 62.

nice, *adj.* silly I 481.

nient, *pron.* nothing, no use I 370.

nier, *v.t.* to deny II 861.

niez, *s.m.* nephew I 1075.

no, *poss.adj.* our I 810.

noces, *s.f.pl.* wedding II Sermon 86.

noiz, *s.f.* nut I 1010.

nombrer, *v.t.* to count II Serventoys estrivé 59.

nonnain, *s.f.* nun I 1065.

nonne, *s.f.* nun I 1044.

nonne, *s.f.* None (Canonical Hour) I 952.

nonpourquant, *adv.* nevertheless I 48.

norrir, *v.t.* to nourish II 579.

nul, *indef. pron.* anyone II 1237.

obscurté, *s.f.* darkness II Serventoys estrivé 40.

octroit, *3rd pers. s. pres. ind.* of *v.t.* **ottroier** (II Sermon 91).

oil, *adv.* yes I 90.

oindre, *v.t.* to annoint II 1170.

oir, *v.t.* to hear I 57.

omme, *s.m.* man II Sermon 59.

onques, *adv.* never I 910.

or, *adv.* now I 949.

ord, *adj.* filthy I 857.

ordener, *v.t.* to put in order II 853.

ore, *adv.* now I 233.

orendroit, *adv.* now II 871.

orreur, *s.f.* stench II Serventoys estrivé 41.

orrez, *2nd pers. pl. fut.* of *v.t.* **oir** to hear II 217.

os, *1st pers. s. pres. ind.* of *v.i.* **oser** to dare II 170.

ostel, *s.m.* home, hostel I 60.

oster, *v.t.* to remove I 44; carry off I 643.

ottroier (otroier), *v.t.* to grant I 226.

ou (en le), *art.* in the II 502; *loc.* **ou mains**, at least I 906.

oultre, *adv.* beyond I 392; *adj.* further II 863.

ouvrer, *v.i.* to act, work I 921.

oy, *p. part.* of *v.t.* **oir** (II 257).

paien, *adj.* pagan, heathen II 346.

painer, *v.refl.* to take pains I 944.

paour, *s.f.* fear I 981.

paoureux, *adj.* fearful I Sermon 14.

pardire, *v.t.* to finish (singing) I 880.

pardurable, *adj.* eternal I 105.

parfaire, *v.t.* to complete, perfect I 91.

parfont, *adj.* learned II 185.

parmy, *prep.* through I 349.

parra, *3rd pers. s. fut.* of *v.i.* **paroir** to show, become visible II 1144.

partroublé, *adj.* extremely troubled I Sermon 34.

pas, *loc.* **le pas**, swiftly II 417.

passage, *s.m.* way past I 928.

peine, *s.f.* trouble, pains II 37.

pener, *v.refl.* to be penitent I 396.

per, *s.m.* peer, equal II Serventoys estrivé 6.

perdicion, *s.f.* perdition I 78.

permanable, *adj.* permanent II 1108.

pers, *s.m.* greenish-blue colour II Sermon 78.

perseverer, *v.i.* to preserve II 697.

pert, *3rd pers. s. pres. ind.* of *v.i.* **paroir** to seem I 833.

peschié, *s.m.* sin I Sermon 58.

peser, *v.t.* to weigh on, distress I 369.

pieça (piece a), *adv.* some time ago I 257.

piteux, *adj.* kind, compassionate II 205.

plaisance, *s.f.* pleasure, delight I 115.

plait, *s.m.* discussion II 370.

planer, *v.t.* to efface II Serventoys estrivé 52.

planté, *s.m.* plenty I 1084.

pleu, *p.part.* of *v.i.* **plaire** to please II 659.

plevir, *v.t.* to pledge I 225.

plonc, *s.m.* lead I 184.

po (pou), *s.m.* little II 818.

poins, *loc.* **de touz poins**, in all ways I 522.

point, *s.m.* situation I 566.

point, *loc.* **a point**, satisfactorily I 246; ready I 607; *loc.* **de point en point**, entirely II 319.

poissance, *s.f.* power II 670.

poissant, *adj.* powerful II Serventoys couronné 18.

porcion, *s.f.* share, allowance II Serventoys estrivé 31.

poucin, *s.m.* young chicken I 538.

pourpre, *s.f.* crimson colour II Sermon 78.

pourvoir, *v.t.* to provide II Serventoys couronné 28.

povoir, *s.m.* power I 372.

predicacion, *s.f.* preaching II 313.

premerain, *adj.* first II 732.

prerogative, *s.f.* prerogative I 111.

prescher, *v.i.* to preach II 348.

preudomme (preudome), *s.m.* worthy man I 85.

prieure, *s.f.* prioress I 94.

prieuresse, *s.f.* prioress I 1039.

prieuse (for prieure), *s.f.* prioress I 55.

prime, *s.f.* first Canonical Hour succeeding Lauds I 30.

principe, *s.m.* beginning II 864.

prisier, *v.t.* to esteem, value I 160.

proier, *v.t.* to beg I 907.

propice, *adj.* propitious, kind II 71.

propos, *s.m.* thought, proposition II 696.

prouver, *v.refl.* to work, put oneself out II 910

pucellage, *s.m.* maidenhood I 223.

pucelle, *s.f.* maiden I 72.

pui, *s.m.* guild II Serventoys estrivé. 56.

purgacion, *s.f.* purification II 1172

quanque, *pron.* and *s.neut.* however much I 130.

querir, *v.t.* to seek II 128.

querre, *v.t.* to seek I 63.

quis, *p.part.* of *v.t.* **querre** to seek II 931.

quittes, adj. absolved I 1069.

raconduire, *v.t.* to bring back I 783.

racorder, *v.refl.* to be reconciled I 851.

rains, *s.m.pl.* loins, back II 1135.

raison, *s.f.* speech, discourse I 87.

raler, *v.i.* to return I 197; *v.refl.* II 1057.

rara, *3rd pers. s. fut.* of *v.t.* **ravoir** to get back II 282.

rebours, *adj.* surly, rebellious II 962.

reçoif, *2nd pers. s. imper.* of **recevoir,** *v.t.* to receive I 825.

reconmander, *v.t.* to recommend II 773.

recordans, *adj.* mindful I 661.

recorder, *v.t.* to recite I 119; *v.refl.* to affirm II 1280.

recors, *s.m.pl.* speech II 1147.

recouvrer, *v.t.* to find I 633; to find what was lost I 1085.

recoy, *s.m.* hiding place I 308.

recueillir, *v.t.* to receive I 706.

redempcion, *s.f.* redemption II 498.

relenquir, *v.t.* to relinquish II 1104.

renier, *v.t.* to renounce II 676.

rente, *s.f.* annuity II 465.

reparacion, *s.f.* restauration I Sermon 49.

reprendre, *v.t.* to blame II 1040.

reputer, *v.refl.* to consider oneself II 374.

requerir, *v.t.* to request I 505.

requerre, *v.t.* to request I 141.

resjoir, *v.t.* to gladden II Serventoys couronné 55.

respit, *s.m.* delay I 618.

respondre, *v.t.* to reply I 1067.

ressoie, *1st pers. s. pres. subj.* of *v.i.* **reestre** to be again I 953.

resusciter (resuciter), *v.refl.* to come back to life II 503.

retraindre, *v.t.* to halt II 633.

retraire, *v.t.* to leave out I 327; to remove from II 316; to save II 1177.

retraiz, *adj.* contracted II 256.

revois, *1st pers. s. pres. ind.* of *v.i.* **raler** to return I 197.

roiz, *s.m.* net, snare II 606.

rondé, *s.m.* rondeau II 327.
rondel, *s.m.* rondeau I 325.
ront, *3rd pers. s. pres. ind.* of *v.t.* **rompre** to break II 62.
roupz, *adj. m.pl.* broken I 152.
rungier, *v.t.* to bite, eat I 537.
ruser, *v.i.* to wait, be made to wait I 170.
ruser, *v.t.* to trick I 375.

sa (ça), *adv.* there I 22.
sain, *s.m.* bosom I 1027.
sain, *adj.* holy II 599.
saindre, *v.t.* to encircle II 646.
saintie, *adj.* f. made holy II Serventoys couronné 4.
saison, *loc.* **il est saisons**, it is time I 293.
salaire, *s.m.* payment II 96.
salutacion, *s.f.* greetings I Sermon 28.
saner, *v.t.* to cure II 593.
santir, *v.t.* to feel, anticipate II Serventoys estrivé 2.
sanz, *prep.* without 355.
sauf, *loc.* **en sauf**, in safety II 1327.
saut, *3rd pers. s. pres. subj.* of *v.t.* **sauver** to save I Sermon 26.
sautier, *s.m.* psalter I 29.
sauvement, *s.m.* salvation II Serventoys couronné 7.
scé, *1st pers. s. pres. ind.* of *v.t.* **sçavoir** to know II 67.
science, *s.f.* learning, knowledge II 248.
seans (ceans), *adv.* here, in this place I 148.
secourre, *v.t.* to help II 1201.
secours, *loc.* **prendre en secours** to save I 893.
seigneurie, *s.f.* power, authority II Serventoys couronné 46.
sejour, *s.m.* delay I 1.
semer, *v.t.* to sow, spread II 888.
sens (senz), *s.m.* good sense II 127.
seoir, *v.refl.* to sit down I 17.
sepmaine, *s.f.* week I 1025.

sepulcre, *s.m.* sepulchre II 502.
sergent, *s.m.* servant II 650.
seri, *adj.* serene, soft I 418.
serrez, *2nd pers. pl. fut.* of *v.refl.* **seoir** to sit down I 713.
servage, *s.m.* slavery II 1157.
service, *s.m.* religious service I 480.
seue, *poss.pron. f.s.* his I 762; *adj.* II 655.
seulz, *2nd pers. s. pres. ind.* of *v.i.* **souloir** to be accustomed I 870.
seur, *adj.* certain I Sermon 16.
seyens see **seans** (I 730).
si, *loc.* **sanz nul si**, without argument II 356.
siecle, *s.m.* earthly life I Sermon 65; world II Serventoys estrivé 29.
siez, *2nd pers. s. imper.* of *v.refl.* **seoir** to sit down I 309.
soing, *s.m.* care II 1158.
solaux, *s.m.* sun II Serventoys couronné 30.
somme, *s.f.* total, all II 311.
songier, *v.i.* to dream II 1345.
songneux, *adj.* careful II 51.
sonner, *v.t.* to proclaim II 537.
soubz, *prep.* beneath II 709.
souffrir, *v.t.* to allow I 854; suffer II 68.
souffrir, *v.refl.* to wait, be patient II 142.
sourdre, *v.i.* to happen, occur I 561.
souspeçonner, *v.t.* to suspect, be suspicious I Sermon 21.
succession, *s.f.* succession, inheritance II Sermon 24.
sueffre, *1st pers. s. pres. ind.* of *v.i.* **souffrir** to suffer II 68; *2nd pers. s. imper.* II 913.
suer, *s.f.* sister I 1.
sus (suz), *adv.* off, away I 34; *prep.* towards I 476.
suspeçon, *s.f.* suspicion I Sermon 42.

tache, *s.f.* spot II 1117.
taire, *v.refl.* to be silent II 1089.

tantait, *s.m.* (*dim.* of **tant**) a little bit I 180.

tantost, *adv.* immediately I Sermon 21.

tarir, *v.t.* to cure, clear up II 637.

tart, *adv.* late I 269.

telz, *adj.* such I 88.

tempoire, *s.m.* time I 872.

temporel, *adj.* worldly II 472.

tendre, *v.i.* to tend to, be near to I 78.

tenir, *v.t.* to hold (lands) I 740; to bind II 374.

tenser, *v.t.* to preserve I 104.

terme, *s.m.* delay I 651.

terre, *s.f.* country, land II 195.

terrien, *adj.* earthly, material I 1093.

tesmoingner, *v.t.* to witness II Sermon 59.

throsne, *s.m.* throne (heavenly) II Serventoys couronné 39.

tiercement, *adv.* thirdly II Sermon 8.

tiers, *adj.* third I 937.

tolir, *v.t.* to prevent, do out of II 1209.

torcher, *v.t.* to wipe I 1029.

torfait, *s.m.* sin, misdeed II 558.

tost, *adv.* soon I 942.

touchier, *v.t.* to mention II Sermon 10.

tour, *loc.* **a nul tour,** in no way I 681.

toutesvoies, *adv.* nevertheless II 560.

traire, *v.t.* to drag out I 181.

traire, *v.refl.* betake oneself I 35.

transitoire, *adj.* transitory II 475.

traveilliez, *adj.* fatigued I 833.

trebuchier, *v.t.* to plunge II 541.

tresoriere, *s.f.* treasurer, guardian I 83.

trespasser, *v.i.* to die II 109.

trespersier, *v.t.* to pierce II Sermon 74.

treuver, *v.t.* to find I 384.

trine, *adj.* triple, of the Trinity II Serventoys estrivé 43.

trop, *adv.* greatly, very I 1074.

troplus, *loc.* **troplus que tant,** utterly II 339.

truant, *s.m.* beggar II 990.

truisse, *3rd pers. s. pres. subj.* of *v.t.* **trouver** to find I 437.

tuit, *adj. m.pl.* all II Serventoys couronné 54.

ueil, *s.m.* eye I 605.

uis see **huis** (I 935).

usage, *loc.* **avoir en usage,** to be accustomed to I 929.

user, *v.t.* to spend I 525.

vair, *s.m.* blue-grey colour II Sermon 79.

valoir, *v.i.* to be of value II 180.

vaulra, *3rd pers. s. fut.* of *v.i.* **valoir** II 302.

veans, *pres. part.* of *v.t.* **veoir** to see I 795.

venin, *s.m.* poison II Serventoys estrivé 53.

veoir, *v.t.* to see I 948.

ver (vair), *adj.* blue-grey, bright I 262.

vergondeux, *adj.* bashful I Sermon 36.

versillier, *v.i.* to recite (verses, prayers) I 459.

vesprée, *s.f.* evening I 476.

vesqui, *3rd pers. s. p. hist.* of *v.i.* **vivre** to live II 577.

vestir, *v.t.* to dress, clothe I 1103.

veu, *s.m.* vow I 1046.

vezcy (vezci: voici), *prep.* see here, behold I 28.

vice, *s.m.* sin II 801.

vilain, *adj.* vile I 889.

vilainement, *adv.* vilely I 859.

vilenie, *s.f.* crime II 765.

vilté, *s.m.* degradation II 889.

virginalment, *adv.* as a virgin, in a virgin way II Serventoys couronné 16.

vis, *s.m.pl.* the living, 'the quick' II 600.

viser, *v.i.* to think, reflect II Serventoys estrivé 23.

vituperer, *v.t.* to vituperate II
Sermon 45.

vo, *poss.adj.* your II 1061.

voiage, *s.m.* journey II 138.

voie (voye), *loc.* se mettre a voie, to
set out I 772.

voire, *adv.* in truth, indeed I Sermon
60.

voirement, *adv.* truly I 382.

voirs, *adj.* true I 545.

vois, 1*st pers. s. pres. ind.* of *v.i.* aler
to go I 98.

voulenté, *s.f.* will I 682.

vuidier, *v.t.* to leave, abandon I 759.

yaue, *s.f.* water I 1064.

ycel (*f.* ycelle), *dem.adj.* that I 134.

yer (ier), *adv.* yesterday I 278.

yla, *adv.* there II 218.

ymage see image (I 406).

ysnel, *adv.* swiftly II 1308; *loc.* ysnel
le pas, swiftly I 473.

ysnellement, *adv.* swiftly I 848.

yssir (issir), *v.i.* to exit, go out I 237.

yst, 3*rd pers. s. pres. ind.* of *v.i.* yssir:
loc. diex yst 'there is no God' I
793.